MW01069142

Praise for

TEACHER BY TEACHER

"In *Teacher By Teacher,* John King powerfully describes not only the ways education saved and shaped his life, but how supporting our teachers can unlock a brighter future for every child everywhere and strengthen democracy itself. This is a must-read book for educators, policymakers, parents, and citizens committed to building a better future."

—Deval Patrick, former Governor of Massachusetts

"I am grateful to John King for sharing his inspirational story and highlighting the true heroes for so many of us."

—Loretta E. Lynch, 83rd Attorney General
of the United States

"Teachers changed my life. Thankfully, they changed John King's as well. *Teacher By Teacher* is proof of the power of an educator—filled with twists, turns, and some of the best that our schools have to offer. Compelling, inspiring, and full of hope."

—Brad Meltzer, #1 *New York Times* bestselling author of
The Lightning Rod

"We are from different parties and have different political perspectives, but John King and I share the unshakeable conviction that education is the path to greater opportunity and prosperity. *Teacher By Teacher* offers important insights into John King's inspiring personal journey, how schools can be structured to successfully close achievement gaps, and what states and the federal government can do to ensure that all children—regardless of race or family income—are prepared to succeed."

—Margaret Spellings, 8th US Secretary of Education and president & CEO of the Bipartisan Policy Center

"Teacher By Teacher is an important book, not just for educators, but for anyone who has an interest in exploring nuanced, innovative, and passionate leadership at all levels—from the classroom to the federal government."

—Kenneth I. Chenault, chairman and managing director, General Catalyst; former chairman and CEO, American Express

THE PEOPLE WHO CHANGE OUR LIVES

TEACHER
BY
TEACHER

JOHN B. KING JR.

LEGACY
LIT

New York Boston

Copyright © 2025 by John B. King Jr.

Cover design by Dana Li. Cover images by Shutterstock and Getty Images. Cover copyright © 2025 by Hachette Book Group, Inc.

Legacy Lit

Hachette Book Group

1290 Avenue of the Americas

New York, NY 10104

hachettebookgroup.com

@LegacyLitBooks

First Edition: April 2025

Legacy Lit is an imprint of Grand Central Publishing. The Legacy Lit name and logo are registered trademarks of Hachette Book Group, Inc.

The publisher is not responsible for websites (or their content) that are not owned by the publisher.

The Hachette Speakers Bureau provides a wide range of authors for speaking events. To find out more, go to hachettespeakersbureau.com or email HachetteSpeakers@hbgusa.com.

Legacy Lit books may be purchased in bulk for business, educational, or promotional use. For information, please contact your local bookseller or the Hachette Book Group Special Markets Department at special.markets@hbgusa.com.

Print book interior design by Amy Quinn

Library of Congress Control Number: 2024952080

ISBNs: 978-1-5387-5777-2 (hardcover), 978-1-5387-5779-6 (ebook)

Printed in the United States of America

LSC-C

Printing 1, 2025

To Melissa, Amina, and Mireya:
Thank you for all your love and support. Our
family is the greatest blessing of my life.

To Mr. Osterweil, Miss D, and all of my amazing teachers and mentors:
Thank you for making my life and career possible. I wake up every
day aspiring to do for other young people what you did for me.

To every teacher and mentor:
Thank you for what you do and who you are in the lives of students.

INTRODUCTION

My first major television interview after becoming US Secretary of Education for President Barack Obama was on *CBS This Morning* with Norah O'Donnell. I asked the TV crew to meet me at P.S. 276 in Canarsie, Brooklyn, a place that defined much of my childhood, my career, and what I believed school should be.

I wasn't new to media attention, but sitting in a classroom that day, I was nervous. I wanted to make all the people who had supported me throughout my academic and professional journey proud and to set the right tone at the start of my time as secretary.

Norah asked rigorous questions about the growing challenge of student debt, the performance of America's schools, and the politics of education. But the conversation wasn't just about policy. As a journalist, she already knew my backstory, that I lost both my parents by the time I was twelve, spent my adolescent years moving between different family members, and ended up getting expelled from high school. My life could have so easily gone in a very different direction, and Norah wasn't the first person curious about my journey. Given all the trauma I had experienced, she wanted to know, how did I earn degrees from Harvard, Columbia, and Yale, and go on to become the first Black and the first Puerto Rican Commissioner of Education for New York State, and serve in President Obama's cabinet?

The answer was simple. I explained that I was blessed to have the right teachers, mentors, and role models, who intervened in my life at the right moments. I am not special, just lucky. I had always worked hard, but so do lots of folks. What made the crucial difference was the generosity of those who chose to teach me, who gave their best in their encounters with me. The ones who could have seen a twelve-year-old boy of color, family in crisis, and asked themselves, *"What chance does he have?"* but instead asked what chance they could give.

Today, the three-story brick building is the same as I remember from my childhood, but behind the black wrought-iron fence, it beckons with a new vibrancy. A forgotten side yard has been transformed into a lush garden with neat rows of herbs, flowers, vegetables, and fruit saplings for the children to tend. Vivid murals with motivational messages adorn the outside walls. A life-size rendering of Dr. George Washington Carver illustrates the scientist's sense of discovery and wonder about the world around him, alongside his words: "Education is the key to unlock the Golden Door of Freedom."

I often urge people who are interested in public policy and the impact of education to visit juvenile justice facilities and prisons to understand folks' journeys. What they would find is that, too often, a life's story is cemented by a split-second decision: A friend asks someone to come along on a trip to the convenience store, then the friend decides to rob the store, and now both are caught up in the system. Wrong time, wrong place. Other times, those impulsive decisions are grounded in deeper traumas with even more tragic consequences. Every life has its turning points. At those critical moments in mine, I was fortunate that there were people who put their hand on my shoulder and made sure I went in the right direction. I feel certain I would be dead or incarcerated if they hadn't.

What has driven my whole career is the knowledge that one teacher showing that they care, providing the right challenge or encouragement, offering the right sage advice or asking the right question, can profoundly change the life of a student. Whether I was teaching high school social studies in Boston or undergraduates at University of Maryland, my goal was to try to do for other young people what teachers had done for me. Whether I was talking with a room of superintendents as commissioner or a room of governors as secretary, my goal was the same: to create more spaces and places where educators could save students' lives the way my teachers had saved mine.

While my story is one of luck, I don't think access to opportunity in American society should depend on luck. I believe we can and should organize our systems to ensure every child has the opportunity to succeed. That is what has defined my career from the classroom to serving in the highest levels of state and federal government. I want to make sure more kids like me get a clear shot at the life I have been blessed to have: a career I am proud of and a family I adore. This is a book about the teachers and the mentors who made that possible for me.

TEACHER
· BY
TEACHER

CHAPTER ONE

I BEGGED TO GO TO SCHOOL THE MORNING MY MOTHER DIED.

I was eight years old and had just spent Halloween night in a hospital waiting room, where everyone kept telling me Mom was all right, that she had just fainted at work. Doctors were going to take care of her, and she would be home soon. She had been fine when she dropped me off at school that morning, and I expected to come home with her and go trick-or-treating. Instead, a friend of hers had appeared to pick me up early from school and take me to Kings County Hospital.

Hospitals weren't unfamiliar to me. Mom had had breast cancer and a mastectomy a year—or was it two?—before, and I saw the scar when we got ready for school together every day. I took it to mean that she was better. Fixed. This time in the waiting room, what felt like endless hours ticked by in slow-motion minutes as I watched doctors and nurses rushing in and out of swinging doors, family members looking up hopefully each time.

I thought I'd get to go beyond the swinging doors to see my mother, but I didn't. All the grown-ups just kept saying everything would be okay, everything would be fine. I was scared, but I believed them. We got home late that night, my hobo costume and empty trick-or-treat bag waiting there, forgotten. I went to bed with the murmured voices of my relatives drifting up from the kitchen, where I found them talking, still, the next morning. I was surprised to see my father, my grandmother, and an aunt—maybe two aunts—sitting around the table; I assumed that meant that my favorite uncle was there somewhere, too. Haldane King was the family's military hero, a Tuskegee Airman who had trained to pilot B-25 bombers during World War II. Usually, if Uncle Hal and my father were under the same roof, you would hear the booming voices of the two brothers jockeying to hold court, and their silence now was more jarring than their noise. So many of the specific details and words of that chilly first day of November have blurred or evaporated altogether over time, but the feeling...more than forty years later, I can still instantly summon the way that morning felt. Muffled, as if an invisible fog had enveloped the whole house that night.

The adults stopped talking when they saw me, quickly herding me into the formal living room we never used. I sat bewildered on the sofa while my father broke the terrible news: "Your mother didn't make it. She died." I remember screaming out for her, the pain beyond anything I could have imagined. I sobbed until I couldn't breathe, and when I had finally calmed down enough to form a thought, to speak, I asked my father a single question: "Where will I go?"

"It'll just be the two of us," he answered. He offered no further comfort or assurances, and I expected none. He was seventy-five years old—older than my maternal grandmother—and we had never had the kind of father-son relationship I saw on my favorite TV shows or read about in storybooks. By the time I had come along in 1975, Dad already had grown grandchildren and was drinking his way through bitter retirement from the career that defined him for over forty years. Both of us depended on Mom's love and vitality to sustain the illusion of normal family life. Still trying to absorb the shock of her being so suddenly gone, I retreated to my bedroom to get dressed and ready for school. I was worried about being late.

"You don't have to go today," my father told me, surprised when I reappeared downstairs with my bookbag.

But I never missed school. I wanted to go. I *needed* to go. School was the sanctuary my mother and I had shared, the cozy snow-globe village where we both thrived, where we felt a part of the world instead of isolated from it in the dark brick house where my father had been slowly deteriorating for years. School was Mom.

Dad had once been esteemed in this same space my mother and I held so sacred. In his prime, John B. King Sr. was a respected, high-ranking educator, a beloved raconteur who turned our brick house in the Flatlands section of Brooklyn into a raucous salon for intellectuals. They kept coming after he stopped working, no one daring to mention Dad's bleary eyes or wandering stories. My mother, Ada, gaily kept the snacks coming, the drinks flowing, and the conversation lively. When she died, I instantly understood that I, too, was now part of denial's unspoken pact when it came to my father. It wasn't as if I had the benefit of comparison to his "good" years, anyway; for as long as I could remember, Dad had been "crazy," and Mom had done her best to buffer me from the worst of his mercurial temper. She taught me by example to tread lightly and keep quiet, how to read the gathering clouds and retreat before the storm hit.

Dad had been drinking and sleeping more than usual in the months before my mother suffered her fatal heart attack at the age of forty-eight, and I used to hear them arguing after I went to bed; I could catch the sharp, low tones but couldn't make out the words. All I knew was that to be in Dad's radius was to be in a constant state of fight-or-flight, and at eight, I was no match for his tirades. My immediate instinct was flight that morning when he announced it would now be "just the two of us," and I begged to go to school until finally someone drove me to P.S. 276 Louis Marshall in Canarsie.

When I first began kindergarten at 276, Mom was the school's guidance counselor. Even after she transferred to the neighborhood's junior high, we rode to school together each morning, listening to Johnny Mathis and other pop stars on the tape deck as we talked about the day ahead. P.S. 276 wasn't my neighborhood school; it was a magnet school with a gifted track called the Astor program, after its benefactor. My classmates and I would stay together each year until sixth grade graduation. The Astor curriculum was designed to land us in one of the city's elite public prep schools, which, in turn, set their top students on a path to the Ivy League and other top-tier colleges and universities. As a counselor, my mother had a front-row purview of the program, and it had impressed her enough to have me tested for a coveted spot in it.

Adalinda King regarded education as more than a career; it was her calling, and the sense of not only purpose but joy that she found in chalk dust, noisy hallways, and students clamoring for attention was imbued in me, as well. School was that exciting place where you sorted out all the mysteries and mayhem of the outside world. I didn't have to be quiet or invisible there. It was safe and exhilarating all at once.

The morning that I lost my mother, Mr. Osterweil was waiting in the hallway outside his classroom. A short, rosy-cheeked man with longish hair, Mr. Osterweil favored three-inch Brazilian platform sandals and patterned shirts in warmer weather, military-style boots and a camel hair greatcoat in the cold, and sunglasses in both. I figured he was a hippie the first time I saw him. Mr. Osterweil treated his pupils like fellow travelers on the same grand adventure, not mere children he was tasked to teach things like pre-algebra and civics during our time together from fourth through sixth grade. He not only asked our opinions about what we were reading or thinking about; he sincerely considered them. His classroom was an amazing place, with its own small library, which Mr. Osterweil had filled with books he bought for us himself, mostly paperbacks. We had the entire *Wizard of Oz* series (my personal favorite), classics like *To Kill a Mockingbird* and *The Swiss Family Robinson*, dictionaries, encyclopedias, and *The Guinness Book of World Records*. The library was constantly growing. The walls of our classroom were papered with colorful maps, and Mr. Osterweil insisted we learn the capital of every state and every country. He told us about trips to Europe and Mexico. He loved beaches, and we learned about mollusks while examining the shells our teacher himself had gathered on beaches he and his wife enjoyed combing on summer vacations. Our desks were all pushed together to form groups. I was chatty and would get reprimanded often for talking to my neighbors. Mr. Osterweil was strict but never mean. I always wanted to please him, to bask in his frequent praise and open approval.

Concern furrowed Mr. Osterweil's brow as I walked down the hall to class that morning after Halloween, and I could tell that he already knew about my mother, which embarrassed me. He told me how very sorry he was and asked, as my father and the principal already had done, if I was sure I wanted to be there that morning. I nodded.

"If you want to talk about it," he gently offered, "we can."

The prospect of that mortified me even more. "We" were a hand-picked collection of pre-adolescent nerds who would have become outcasts in the mainstream but together constituted a bold coalition of sorts, small Baltic states willing to fight for each other to the bitter end while desperately hoping no one ever challenged us to do so. But I didn't want solidarity or comfort that day; it would, in fact, take decades for me to overcome this newfound dread. I took my usual seat next to my best friend, Dale—like me, one of the few Black males in our class—and said nothing about what had happened, not even to him.

In turn, my classmates afforded me what, for fourth graders, was the greatest dignity of all—never asking me why I had been crying though it was all too obvious I had been. I pretended to be engrossed in the *New York Times* I had picked up from the stack Mr. Osterweil put by the classroom door for us each morning. Combat between American and Cuban forces continued on the tiny island of Grenada. Argentine elections had ousted the Peronists. There were 700,000 potholes in New York City, a giant species of rat in Sumatra, a memorial service for the famed ballet choreographer George Balanchine. An earthquake in Turkey had killed nearly a thousand people overnight.

I know now that it was more than a rote response that pulled me to the school in my saddest hour. It was something much deeper: the survival instinct of a broken child. A heart's muscle memory. My life, overnight, had become untethered, drifting alongside me like a balloon about to sail away forever if I didn't grab for the fragile string that would reconnect us. School always felt so *clear* to me. It was rigorous and challenging, supportive, dependable, and reassuring. Things outside of school were not clear. All I wanted this single Tuesday to be was normal. If it could be normal, I could go on being the same boy I was the day before, and the day before that. I didn't know how to be *that boy without a mother*. You could study every book in the world and not be prepared for that test.

Having informed me of my mother's death, my father considered the subject closed.

I didn't doubt that he was grieving, too, but our pain was divided into individual plots to tend alone. Knowing no better, I assumed this was how it worked. You keep your screams to yourself. Dad didn't take me to the funeral. This, too, I assumed was mandated by some kind of rule. My half brother, Gil, described the service to me afterward, recounting how Mom's junior high students stood at her gravesite crying. I knew that the kids she dealt with most often were the troubled ones, the tough kids she used to ask my father how to best handle in his better days. Now they were the ones who got to say goodbye. It only underscored how unfair losing her felt to me.

In those first few weeks without her, the house was always full, friends and family streaming through with food and more food, an endless buffet we barely touched. The reality of what "just the two of us" would be like didn't immediately sink in

7

with the doorbell constantly ringing. Gil had to return to college and his Long Island bachelor pad, but our maternal grandmother came every weekend to stay and keep me company. On the King side of the family, my half sister Lynne checked on her father often at first, but always brought her husband, a plainclothes undercover cop who lived conspicuously beyond his means and had a thuggish, intimidating air about him as he leaned against his latest Mercedes. My other half sister, Joan, was less present. I recognized other familiar faces at the kitchen table like Slim and Evelyn, a couple who had been regular fixtures in my parents' social life, their best friends. Former colleagues of both my father and my mother also stopped by. A polite "fine" was the only answer I knew to give anyone who might ask how I was doing.

How—or even if—we marked the holidays without my mother that year is lost to me. I've since learned that children who've been traumatized often lose great swaths of memory and have difficulty building new ones. The best I can do is retrieve random pieces and shards from my childhood, my life story a mosaic, not a puzzle.

We usually celebrated Thanksgiving at Lynne's house in Great Neck and stayed in Brooklyn for Christmas. I held on to warm memories of both. In Great Neck, I liked to slip away by myself into the living room, where I would settle onto a big sofa with puffy cushions to pick the peanuts and raisins that I favored out of the snack bowl left out on the coffee table. Christmas in Brooklyn meant gifts under the tree, stockings hung from the mantel, and mesmerizing storytelling by my father. Listening to him recount how the iceman used to deliver blocks of ice and other "olden days" tales from his childhood is still one of my fondest memories of him. His stories usually had a fable-like quality to them, with some moral to take away about hard work or patience.

One of the fullest and most comforting memories I have from those years after my mother died is of my Uncle Hal and Aunt Jean's house in New Jersey. I loved the cacophony of that home, so unlike ours, with jazz playing and little kids chasing each other through the house shrieking, and the grown-ups all crowded in the kitchen, laughing and talking as delicious aromas wafted from Aunt Jean's oven. When it was warm enough outside, people would be in the backyard pool or hovering around the barbecue. My dad and Uncle Hal were the only siblings left from a large but tragic family, and close despite an age gap big enough to make Dad more like a father figure to Hal. Dad was nearly fourteen when Hal was born; there were five brothers in all, and two sisters, though I was told the oldest son, Charlie, and his brother Eddie fell into the mobster life and either died young or got killed. I was a random twig on the family tree: The first cousins I knew growing up were inevitably much older while their kids—my first cousins once removed—were much younger than I was. I would sometimes entertain the younger ones at the kids' table during family gatherings, but I would just as often join the conversation at the adult table. I had my fair share of opinions about current events, thanks to Mr. Osterweil's classroom. (My precociousness was tolerated graciously at our holiday gatherings, though family lore now pegs me as having been something of a little know-it-all.) Sometimes, that first year after losing Mom, Dad would drive us to New Jersey on a random weekend, just to go visit Hal and Jean.

After the holidays, the stream of visitors slowed to a trickle, and by the time I turned nine in January, my father was spending more time alone in his bedroom. Much of my mother's belongings were untouched. Her jewelry box still sat atop the dresser. Every morning, Dad would get up to drive me to school and then come back to pick me up in the afternoon, but there was an empty silence now where Johnny Mathis once sang and Mom once chatted. I was surprised one weekend morning when Dad announced that we needed to go to the nursery. Spring gardening had always been one of Mom's joys. Dad had planted tidy rows of rosebushes in the small garden behind our house. He chose identical shades of red, pink, and white flowers. Mom had triumphantly disrupted his sense of order by planting a single bush in her favorite color, yellow. Now, as I helped my father carry the bags of fertilizer, gardening tools, and flats of impatiens and geraniums to the flower beds, I felt a surge of hope that he was trying, that maybe we would get used to each other and do things together now. But the only conversation was about what to rake or prune next.

Spring brought other disappointments, too: After finishing my homework, I would usually play ball in the street with two boys from the block, white brothers named Heath and Jason, who went to the neighborhood's P.S. 203 and belonged to Little League teams. Seeing them in their uniforms had always filled me with envy. I coveted that uniform and what it stood for. My yearning for that uniform was as palpable as a hunger pang. I wanted to show the world that I *belonged* to something like that, a baseball or basketball or even soccer team. And as deeply as I yearned for it, I also understood that it was a fantasy, something that would never happen in my shrinking world.

Even before Mom's death, our detached brownstone was always dimly lit, the air inside rank with Dad's cigarette smoke and dark mood swings. Now, with my mother no longer there to serve as our bridge, my father and I went about our separate lives under the same roof, the oppressive silence broken only when Dad was lucid enough to ask about my grades or drunk enough to go on one of his rampages. If Heath and Jason weren't around after school, I'd ride my bike around the neighborhood beneath the broad shade of the plane trees or busy myself setting up elaborate battlegrounds in a corner of our unused dining room with my G.I. Joes and baggies full of plastic army men. Dad and I would eat dinner at the kitchen table in front of the TV, watching the evening news. He never asked what I thought about the Cold War or Ronald Reagan or the war in El Salvador like Mr. Osterweil did. Dad would clean up the dishes and disappear back into his room, the door closed behind him, while I watched my favorite sitcoms (some new, some reruns)—*The Cosby Show, Family Ties, Diff'rent Strokes, The Jeffersons, All in the Family.*

At first, Dad would drive to the bank every Saturday or every other Saturday and get an envelope of cash, which he would keep in his bureau and use for groceries, cigarettes, bottles of liquor, or a rare tank of gas for our mostly idle car. We would go shopping together for food, relying mostly on simple things. Cereal, milk, frozen TV dinners in compartmentalized tin trays, cans of spaghetti. I missed my mother's pork chops, but I could easily replicate the white bread and cheese sandwich and bag of potato sticks she used to pack me for lunch each school day. She always made sure I had money for the ice cream truck that parked every afternoon outside P.S. 276's vast blacktop, waiting for the recess bell to ring and all the kids to line up for Popsicles or Fun Dip (basically a pouch with a couple of compartments full of brightly colored sugar and a dipping stick also made out of sugar, which horrifying as it sounds, I loved).

I never went inside Heath and Jason's house, and they didn't ask to come inside mine. This didn't strike me as strange, though, since our stretch of East Forty-Ninth Street had never been the block-party type anyway. When my father had bought the house during his first marriage, sometime in the 1940s or '50s, there had been some organized opposition to selling to a Black family. The Holocaust survivor next door was said to have started a petition and applied enough pressure for the sale to go through. Many of the houses had changed hands in the ensuing years, but we were still one of just a few Black families on the block amid Jewish and Italian families, along with some Cubans. I considered myself Puerto Rican then, like my mother. Still, I never experienced any racism nor felt any hostility on our block; it was more like everyone kept to themselves. The Italians across the street had huge, boisterous Sunday dinners with dozens of extended family members every week after Mass, everyone hugging and kissing as each guest arrived as if it had been decades—not merely the previous Sunday—since they'd last gathered. The Cubans liked to gather outdoors to celebrate nice weather with music playing and grills smoking. But more than ethnicity, socioeconomic status, religion, or anything else, what defined my family and shaped its identity was education.

The classroom was where my parents met and fell in love. At the time, Dad was retired from the New York Board of Education but had returned to teaching as a professor at Fordham University, where Adalinda Garcia was his graduate student. Dad was a widower with two adult daughters. Joan and Lynne were around the same age as Ada, a pretty divorcee born in Ponce, Puerto

Rico, with a teenage son of her own. Hers was a classic "Nuyorican" story. She came to the Bronx at five, learned English in the New York City public schools, and went to Hunter College as the first in her family to go to college.

Neither King daughter approved of the professor's May-December romance. My mother's family disliked the twenty-six-year age gap between student and professor as well, but there was no denying John King's success and bearing. His career would have been considered remarkable under any circumstance, but for a Black American who had to endure a deeply segregated New York City, the Great Depression, and decades of entrenched racism in every segment of American society, his trajectory was nothing short of extraordinary.

Even if I didn't yet grasp the extent of his accomplishments, I was reminded on a daily basis just how important he had been: Up the six wide marble steps and just inside the front to P.S. 276, near the fire extinguisher, hung a small plaque engraved with my father's name as one of the senior officials for New York City public schools when the school was built. The plaque didn't mention that he was the first Black man to reach the rank of executive deputy superintendent—second-in-command of the world's largest public school system. First Black Man was a recurring title on the superachiever side of the King family; the other side included criminals, addicts, and ne'er-do-wells who were rarely if ever seen, invited, or mentioned at family gatherings, though Uncle Hal, a great believer in second chances, would quietly take in different relatives who needed a restart over the years. No one would have guessed back then that I would one day become one of them.

In the 1920s, when Dad came of age, high school was generally the preserve of well-off white boys. Most working-class

white families made their sons get jobs and turn over their pay-
checks once they finished middle school. In Black families,
that usually happened after grade school. But my father, whose
great-grandfather had been born into slavery, was destined
to break loose of whatever or whoever tried to bind him. He
entered Boys' High School in Brooklyn at thirteen and graduated at fifteen with dreams of going to college to become a doctor. When he realized what a burden a medical education would
place on his parents with such a large family to support on his
father's wages as a porter and his mother's earnings from taking
in laundry, Dad abandoned his dream and hired on at a stove
factory. He worked double shifts there before attending night
classes at the City College of New York. His work ethic and
intelligence so impressed the white factory owner that he offered
to pay for his young employee's further education.

Around this same time, though, Dad's father died at
fifty-one, increasing the pressure for Dad to find a way to help
provide for his mother and younger siblings. He responded to
an ad on the subway seeking teachers and, at his benefactor's
urging, enrolled at the prestigious Maxwell Training School for
Teachers. Dad became a substitute teacher just after his twentieth birthday, and he got his own classroom three years later,
once the Depression had eased and schools were able to hire
full-time teachers again. Along the way, Dad also returned to
school to earn both a bachelor's and a master's from NYU.

For thirty-nine years, he steadily climbed the professional ladder, earning a PhD in the process and never once missing a day's
work. One of the few stories about his past that my father ever
told me—and everyone else—was about the time he broke his
wrist one weekend while playing basketball with his younger

brother, William, known as "Dolly," a star athlete who won All-American honors in college and later was among the first Black players in what is today's National Basketball Association.

When Dad went to work that Monday sporting a cast, the principal told him to go home until his wrist healed; school regulations forbade teaching with a cast. "That doesn't make sense," my father argued. "I can teach!"

The principal wouldn't budge. "It's policy," he insisted.

With that, my father walked over to a nearby counter, slammed his cast down, then brushed away the shattered pieces of plaster before heading to his classroom, keeping his swollen hand tucked in his pocket while he taught.

Years after his wrist had fully healed, he still would occasionally hold it up, give it a thoughtful rub, and predict rain the next day. The famous wrist was as useful in child psychology as it was in meteorology—when Dad thought I was slacking off in any way, all he had to do was hold it up, and I would get the unspoken message: In this family, you soldier on.

I knew as a child how important my father had once been, but I only discovered how charismatic and deeply admired he was long after he was gone, when I came across a chapter devoted to him while thumbing through an obscure book published in 1970 titled *Negroes of Achievement in Modern America*. I learned that Dad had retired when his first wife died four years into his job as deputy superintendent. He talked about looking forward to spending more time with his grandchildren. But grief unsettled him, and it wasn't long before he took the professorship at Fordham to find solace in the classroom. It was where he felt normal again.

My father already had a whole family, a career, a separate life before he married Mom and I came into the picture. I was always at the edge of the frame. He was much older than the other dads, more like a sour grandfather, his mind beginning to fade just as mine was ready to blossom. Even as his undiagnosed dementia took hold, Dad was an imposing man who always carried himself as if he were in a suit and tie. He could be wearing pajamas and still look like he was wearing a suit. That formal bearing made his unexplained decline even more impactful, even when Mom was around to provide a smokescreen.

When my mother was alive and friends and relatives were still visiting regularly, the raconteur they all remembered from the old days would sometimes emerge briefly. I hovered with my own sense of anticipation, hoping this would be one of the times Dad would start bragging about what a great student I was, urging me to go fetch a report card or tell our guests about something I was working on. Those were the times when I felt like he noticed me, maybe even believed I had the same mettle as his grandson, Keith, who was about fifteen years older than I was and had attended Cornell and Howard University College of Medicine on his journey to eventually becoming a nationally renowned nephrologist. Dad used to regularly tell me how very proud he was of Keith, how Keith as a kid would be out playing basketball with his friends and someone would pass the ball to Keith, and it would just bounce off the court. Everyone would be looking around, *Where'd Keith go?* Then someone would check their watch—*Ahhhh, it's four thirty, Keith's gone to do homework.* No one had to tell Keith what to do; he was doing it or finished before they even thought to. If my father had any stories like that about me, I never heard them. His interest in me was always fleeting, a ball that never stayed in play long. His focus was limited to what I was achieving, never what I was thinking. I quashed any curiosity I had about his life, or even childish questions about life in general, for that matter, for fear of making him mad. We both loved sports, but he was too old and grouchy to come outside to play with me. Sometimes we would find ourselves watching a basketball or baseball game on TV, sitting side by side, but it didn't feel like we were doing it together, and we never talked sports.

Every day at school was filled with talk, overflowing with questions, answers, ideas, debate about the famine in Ethiopia or the nuclear accident at Chernobyl or the first meeting between President Reagan and Soviet leader Mikhail Gorbachev. Unlike my dad, Mr. Osterweil couldn't wait to discuss everything. The class would study current events and social issues—human rights, world hunger, nuclear proliferation—then ponder solutions. When Mr. Osterweil called on us in class, he wasn't looking for an answer as much as an explanation. He wanted to know what we thought, not just what we knew, his eyes twinkling as if we were enlightening him, not the other way around.

A lover of the arts, Mr. Osterweil would have us stage skits reenacting peace talks in the Middle East for civics class, then pivot to playing out scenes from our literature books for English. He loved to stage elaborate plays that stretched our reading skills and our acting chops. I was the rose in the garden scene in *Alice in Wonderland*, and the priest who married off the couples at the conclusion of *A Midsummer Night's Dream*—a character and plot twist that sprang from Mr. Osterweil's imagination, not Shakespeare's.

Following your imagination was a lesson Mr. Osterweil was more inclined to teach by example than by book or lesson plan. The first time he took us to the Brooklyn Botanic Garden, Mr.

Osterweil suddenly shouted with glee: *Let's run!* Off he went, platform sandals and all, leading us in a loop around the curated trees, bushes, and flowers. Field trips were frequent and always exciting, often with Mr. Osterweil's two little girls joining us. I listened to arias at the Metropolitan Opera, watched ballerinas pirouette across the stage at Lincoln Center, saw *The Taming of the Shrew* at the Shakespeare Theatre in Stratford, Connecticut. In the three years we spent together, Mr. Osterweil never ran out of things he wanted to show us, share with us, so much knowledge and wonder he wanted to seep into our very pores.

————

I was eleven when Dad abruptly stopped going to the store. First one Saturday went by without our usual grocery run, then another.

The cupboards and refrigerator grew barer by the day. The stack of TV dinners in the freezer grew shorter and then were gone. I ate the last of the Cinnamon Life cereal without milk and then there wasn't any food left in the house. Truly none at all. I kept waiting for us to go to the grocery store. Dad went to the bank as usual, but he didn't seem to be hungry or even know whether it was time for dinner or breakfast. He just stayed in his room, sleeping or drinking or smoking.

I wasn't on any meal program at school—we wouldn't have qualified as low-income—and my stomach growled as I watched my classmates eat at lunchtime. I grew desperately hungry, but I didn't tell anyone. If I wanted to eat, I realized I could no longer just wait for Dad to have a good day and act. I could tell he was already beyond that, even though I had no idea why. He was just "crazy," and that was a shameful secret I had always kept.

"Crazy" wasn't something you talked about; you just accepted it and made do.

When he yanked me out of bed at two in the morning and said I was late for school and had to go right now, I screamed, "No, Daddy, no! It's not time!" and clung to the banister with all my might until he gave up and let go. When he burst in waving a chair over his head while I was doing homework and tried to beat me with it, I blocked him with my own chair. When he started kicking over the battlefield tableau I had spent days creating with my G.I. Joes in a corner of the dining room, then kicked harder and faster as I scrambled to scoop up the tiny soldiers and stuff them back into their plastic baggies, I told myself he didn't mean to kick me, as well. He was my father. If he was angry at me, it was my fault for making a mess. But just watching, waiting, and hoping for a reprieve, for a flash of normalcy, were no longer options for me.

At some point, I knew, Dad would emerge from his room and make his way downstairs, most likely infuriated over some imaginary wrong. Simply saying "Good morning" carried a risk that I would be berated for being disrespectful. I was a terrible son, I was regularly reminded, a terrible disappointment to him.

One day, I waited in my room until I heard his footsteps on the stairs, then I slipped into his forbidden bedroom. Slowly, quietly, I opened the top dresser drawer, the one where I had seen him put away his weekly withdrawals from the bank. I was astonished to find the drawer stuffed with tiny white envelopes still full of cash. There were dozens of them. I quickly stuffed some into my pocket and walked a few blocks to the store, filling my basket with boxes of macaroni and cheese, cans of Chef Boyardee, hot dogs, eggs, and a jug of strawberry soda. I felt like I was stealing from my father even as I made him dinner that evening. I was a thief, ashamed of myself, but I had no choice.

I kept going back for more envelopes when we ran out of things. I needed to buy detergent so I could do the laundry. Binder paper for school. Dad had stopped driving altogether, but P.S. 276 now had a van to pick up its far-flung Astor students. I walked to a local bodega after school to get myself grapes and strawberry soda every day. I loved grapes.

People spending an hour or so with Dad on what passed for a good day might not catch on to how seriously ill he was, but I had reason to assume the rest of my family knew even if they said nothing to me. No one gave his behavior a name or spoke of it.

Once when my grandmother was staying for the weekend, I woke up early to the sound of water sloshing and crept downstairs to find the kitchen flooded, my father standing naked and disoriented at the overflowing sink, where he was trying to wash dishes along with a New York City phone book. My grandmother woke up and saw it, too. Dad said nothing and stalked out of the room when he saw us. We mopped up the mess and talked about anything except what we had just witnessed.

On Fridays, my half brother, Gil, would often pick me up to come hang out with him for the weekend and live the life of a twenty-something, which felt like a whole summer vacation wrapped in two days. But the visitors always left, the friends dwindled away, and the outings my relatives orchestrated always ended with me back home alone to care for both me and my father. I remember the pain in the pit of my stomach that flared on each drive home from my brother's apartment after a weekend on Long Island. I never asked him to stop, to turn around and take me back to his place to stay. My home life was the secret everyone knew. I assumed someone would be rescuing me any day.

My bedroom window looked down on the back courtyard of a family that lived one block over. A father, a mother, and a son and daughter. The little courtyard had a patio table and chairs, and a grill. In pleasant weather, I could see the father grilling, the mother bringing out dishes or placing an icy pitcher of lemonade on the table, the teen children laughing and joking as everyone sat down for a happy supper. On the evenings when they weren't outside, I could see the warm lamplight in their windows, and I would imagine the cozy togetherness inside, everyone watching a favorite show on TV, or maybe they were just getting home and settling in after cheering one of the kids on at a high school game. They said good night and I love you before turning off the lights.

Our house was paid for, but bills began piling up in the mail my father never opened. The overdue ones often bore bold warnings like URGENT! stamped on their envelopes. Once I mustered the nerve to open some, I found that the electricity and water would be turned off if they weren't paid. The bills always included clear, simple instructions about how to pay what was owed, so I stole my father's checkbook and added forgery to my list of survival crimes. I rummaged around his papers when he was asleep until I found one with his signature, which I carefully traced over and over again on onion skin paper, until I was sure I could copy it. The fact that it was my name, too, made it seem less deceitful somehow when I signed my first check.

I signed my own permission slips for field trips to the Brooklyn Academy of Music, where we watched a dance performance, and to the Cloisters Museum, where we were transported to the

Middle Ages, full of new possibilities for my beleaguered G.I. Joes and their plastic platoons.

From field trips to classroom discussions, Mr. Osterweil showed us how to learn about the world by engaging with it. I debated nuclear disarmament with my academic arch-rival, Jason Cooper, and chose the hardest nation—the Soviet Union—for a social studies project. That spring, in my sixth grade year, an eleven-year-old Soviet girl with green eyes and a blond pageboy visited the United States on a whirlwind tour to promote "peace and friendship." Katya Lycheva's 1986 trip was also intended to honor the legacy of a ten-year-old schoolgirl from Maine who had made history a few years earlier after penning a heartfelt appeal for world peace to Soviet leader Yuri Andropov. To the world's surprise, the Communist Party chief replied, assuring Samantha Smith that no one in the USSR wished for war. He invited Sam and her parents to visit. Their extraordinary tour behind the Iron Curtain made international headlines, and the fifth grader became a celebrity, a junior peace activist, and a budding actress with a role on a new children's show. Just the summer before, Sam and her father were flying home on a rainy night after filming for *Lime Street* when their small commuter plane crashed, killing all eight people aboard. Now Mr. Osterweil's classroom was one of the first stops in America for Katya, whose tour would also include visits to the circus, McDonald's, Disneyland, and the White House, where she would shake President Reagan's hand. We were fidgeting with excitement as TV crews and newspaper reporters—both Soviet and American—crowded into our classroom along with Katya, her mother, a translator, and stony-faced chaperones. (KGB agents, our next morning's edition of the *New York Times* would inform us.)

Katya told us about the Soviet children's organization Young Pioneers and showed us photos of Moscow, where she lived with her parents, then we were invited to ask questions. Of course, Jason Cooper's hand shot up, and he was called on. Jason wanted to know what Katya had learned in school about the United States. Katya glanced at her translator and replied that those studies were "for later." I'm not sure whether I was too shy, too slow off the mark with my hand, or just hoping to look cooler than Jason, but I failed to get a question in. I'd never met a real Communist before, and the visit was too short (and the Q and A session shorter still) to find out much about the way Katya's life differed from ours. It was the kind of day that made me loneliest for my mother, who would have been full of questions for me about our visitors, and what I thought. I went home instead to my father's oppressive silence and unpredictable outbursts. It was never going to get better, I was beginning to realize. This was my life. Who else would take care of him?

I tamped down dreams of my own future self with a normal life, a family, maybe going to law school, maybe becoming someone who could change the world. I found refuge instead in the borrowed lives of books. I read my way through the shelves of books in Mr. Osterweil's library and my parents' vast and eclectic collection at home. When I pulled the dictionary out from the shelves at home, I could see tiny checkmarks—at least three after every word—in my father's handwriting. I later read in *Negroes of Achievement in Modern America* that he had read the dictionary to prepare for the teacher's exam when he was in his teens. It was in the books that I could see my father clearest.

I didn't know what would come after sixth grade graduation. Leaving Mr. Osterweil's world was pushing me farther out into a scary unknown. My half sister Lynne brought Dad to the graduation ceremony, and he was good that morning. Jason and I had been tied for top student, and I ended up getting to deliver the commencement speech while Jason got the principal's award. I spoke about all we had learned and experienced as a class. After the ceremony, Lynne took us out to eat. It felt good, normal, and I kept telling myself that my father felt proud of me. I'm not sure anymore whether it really happened or if I just wished it into my memory, but when the waitress came to take our order, he boasted that his son was valedictorian.

Lynne dropped us home and then it was "just the two of us" again, and Mr. Osterweil's class was gone forever. The family in the courtyard appeared more often in the long, soft twilights of June as I watched them from my window. I think it must have been around then that the thought first entered my mind. There *was* an end to this, I thought. I could end it all.

CHAPTER TWO

My new school, Mark Twain Junior High School 239 for the Gifted & Talented in Coney Island, was an hour's bus ride and an entire galaxy away from the cocoon of P.S. 276 and Mr. Osterweil's classroom. Admission to the prestigious public magnet school was selective, and one of the requirements was to have a "talent" to cultivate. There were "tracks" at Mark Twain for students who excelled at creative writing, say, or visual arts, or math, or science, for example. I wasn't sure how talented I was at creative writing, but I had always earned good grades, and I enjoyed it, so I applied for that track and was duly enrolled. My buddy Dale would be attending Mark Twain, too, but he had opted for a different track. When I stepped off the bus that first day, I was a stranger in a strange land.

It's a swift and brutal fall from being a sixth grade know-it-all atop the gentle hill of elementary school to a seventh grade nobody at Kilimanjaro's base camp. Threading my way through halls teeming with actual teenagers, I knew there wouldn't be an ice cream truck waiting for me at lunchtime anymore. Instinct told me that finding my place on the sprawling campus on Neptune Avenue—blocks from the famous boardwalk and historic Cyclone—would come down to finding the right teacher, and the right classroom. This was no idle mission: I was eleven years old that fall and, for all intents and purposes, parentless. School was literally the only thing I could be hopeful about anymore, the only thing I could look forward to. School had taken the place of home, in my heart. I was keen to take root somewhere in Mark Twain's mazelike beige brick building, to recapture some of the security I had felt in the Astor program. As luck, or maybe destiny, would have it, I instantly found that sweet spot when I walked into my social studies class.

Celestine DeSaussure was the first Black teacher I ever had. A force of nature, Miss D was the strict but benevolent monarch of a squirrelly tween realm. Dark-skinned, with a cropped Afro and a radiant smile, Miss D was probably in her thirties, maybe forties, and she exuded a warmth that belied her regal bearing; if someone were playing her in a movie, Viola Davis would be cast, no question.

Like Mr. Osterweil, Miss D had lofty expectations for us, but they came with generous helpings of praise and encouragement. She wanted more from us because she believed in us. Our intelligence and worth were presumed. She also shared Mr. Osterweil's flair for theatrics—and then some. Miss D was, in fact, an actress. She had earned her master of fine arts in theater and acting from Cornell and had appeared in numerous plays and regional theater productions before devoting herself to education. Her background made her a spellbinding storyteller. Miss D knew how to make history come alive, her expressive voice transporting us effortlessly from Cleopatra's court to the Cold War, often with no rest stops along the way.

She assigned us a project with each unit, and she expected to see imagination, not just information. I was eager to please her and threw myself into my first big project—the Aztecs—as if the assignment had come straight from the Smithsonian. We were tasked with creating an Aztec news channel, and I nailed my role as sports anchor with my report on tlachtli, the Mesoamerican version of basketball, where opposing teams try to pass a rubber ball through stone hoops using only their hips, thighs, and forearms. The sport offered plenty of fodder for my color commentary, since games were used to flaunt social class, honor the gods, and settle disputes. Tlachtli also served as basic training to prepare for war and as a pregame ritual for human sacrifice. The class loved my broadcast—what audience wouldn't be thrilled and horrified by a pickup ball game ending with decapitation?—and I earned an A.

In Miss D's room, I also felt my first flicker of Black pride. I had never seen a teacher who openly challenged the way American society operated and the system of power that supported it. Miss D's passion for critical thinking planted seeds of discomfort with American inequity in my own mind. My love of debate and Miss D's willingness to engage (or maybe indulge me) quickly earned me special status among my classmates. If someone hadn't done their homework or wasn't prepared for a quiz, I was deployed to take Miss D off subject to stall for time. It didn't take me long to discover that President Reagan was Miss D's Achilles' heel. Fortunately, it didn't take much more than a seventh grade education to mount an argument for Reaganomics. I would light the fire with an innocent question, my hand shooting into the air at an appropriately inopportune time—within minutes of the dismissal bell, or when we could sniff a pop quiz in the air.

"Miss D? Aren't tax cuts for wealthy investors good for the economy? Because tax cuts help business, right?" I remember asking as earnestly and innocently as my own acting skills would allow.

Supply-side economics was a topic I knew Miss D couldn't resist. As usual, she would answer with a question of her own, meant to provoke deep thought.

"And so does everyone benefit from that?" she prompted me.

"Well, yeah, because ultimately the economy grows," I replied triumphantly. Case closed, win to John.

Ever the actress, Miss D managed to hold her indignation in check.

"Does everyone get a share?" she demanded.

If I timed it right, the dismissal bell would save me from annihilation-by-argument.

Even with the Aztecs, Miss D wanted us to dig deep and think about how societies were structured, about who had power and how they chose to wield it.

Outside class, I had moved on in my leisure reading to the dog-eared books that I found on the shelves in Gil's old room. There was also a TV there, and I often fell asleep on my brother's bed after watching *The Odd Couple, Barney Miller, Sanford and Son*, or some other favorite sitcom. It didn't take long before I made the shift from squatter to land grabber, claiming the room—and Gil's library—as my own. I soon found myself deep in the radical pages of *The Autobiography of Malcolm X, Manchild in the Promised Land*, and the one that resonated the deepest, *Down*

These Mean Streets by Piri Thomas. Thomas was a half-Puerto-Rican, half-Cuban Afro-Latino writer and poet whose memoir told the story of growing up in Spanish Harlem. I was excited to read something in the voice of someone like me, grappling with race and identity in a society that so often systemically treated dark-skinned boys with contempt.

My earliest memory of the othering and diminishing that still too often accompanies being Black or brown in America came in kindergarten, the day a classmate sent me home in tears by telling me my skin looked dirty. A sense of shame and sadness intensified deep in my chest each time she repeated the word "dirty," pointed at my skin, and giggled.

"You're not dirty," my mother soothed me when I told her the story that night. "You're beautiful. Your skin is the color of cinnamon."

My self-esteem was instantly restored. Cinnamon was my favorite flavor; I ate a bowl of Cinnamon Life cereal every morning. My mother's love served as part of a family ethos of optimism about America's potential and progress, and my integrated school environment at P.S. 276 created largely positive firsthand experiences of racial diversity for me at a tender age.

But racial reckoning gets harder as you get older. From the windows of P.S. 276, my elementary school had an unfiltered view of racial strife in junior high when it was time to go home and police vans would regularly be waiting across the street outside Bildersee Junior High School in anticipation of fights between white, Black, and Puerto Rican groups of students. When sixth grade graduation loomed, I worried that I might soon find myself a bloodied bystander in some similar ongoing battle, if that was the inevitable trajectory of the transition to junior high school. I wasn't looking forward to a descent into near daily tribal conflicts.

Fortunately, the diverse student body (integrated by court order years earlier) and faculty at Mark Twain J.H.S. formed a more functional multicultural community with the "talent" groups helping to create strong cross-racial bonds. But I was learning daily about conflicts involving race from the world around me.

Throughout my childhood, watching the local news at 5:00, 5:30, and again at 6:00 and then the national nightly news broadcast at 6:30, was a standard routine. Even as my father seemed less and less tethered to reality, habits stayed with him, and sitting in the kitchen watching the news was one. The news—especially the New York City local news of the 1980s—provided a steady stream of harrowing racial tensions. There was the 1984 subway shooting when a white man named Bernie Goetz felt threatened by a group of young Black men and shot all four, arguing later that he thought he was about to be robbed. The shooting provoked a fierce, often racialized debate about soaring crime and vigilantism. Then came the Howard Beach incident in 1986 when a Black man's car broke down in a predominantly white neighborhood and a mob—who didn't think he "belonged" there—chased him onto the Belt Parkway, where he was killed by an oncoming car. Growing into my tween years, I wondered sometimes if I was safe in my cinnamon skin and what would happen to me if I was perceived as a threat or thought to be in the wrong place at the wrong time.

Political ads at the time seized onto the phrase "Morning in America" to trumpet the national economic recovery from recession, evoking images of everyone (white) waking to sunshine and good cheer. But the trusty evening news had a very different camera trained on African-Americans, who featured prominently in stories about poverty, overcrowded shelters, and the ravages of the emerging crack epidemic.

What I saw raised vexing questions, which I pondered alone in Gil's room, the serenity of its blue walls a sharp contrast to my churning adolescent mind. Why were things so unequal? Why hadn't Dr. King's "dream" that we read about in elementary school been fully realized? Why was race such a trigger for conflict? There was no trusted parent or sibling to ask how the color of my skin factored into not just the world around me, but the world waiting for me.

My new reading list was helping me explore these questions, to understand America's history around race more deeply, and to begin to see my place in it. I was accustomed to leading with my Puerto Rican identity. I knew from overheard adult conversations, the banter of my brother's college friends, and the cultural zeitgeist I had internalized from television that somehow being Puerto Rican was less threatening, less prone to rejection, than being Black. But as I grappled with critiques of America's racial inequality, engaged with authors whose experiences more closely mirrored my own (especially Thomas's descriptions of the intersections of ethnicity and skin color), and enjoyed having my first Black teacher, I grew increasingly confident about asserting my Blackness alongside my Puerto Rican identity. The jokes on shows like Good Times, Sanford and Son, and The Jeffersons also began to land differently. I delighted in the humanity, the dignity, and the silliness just as much, but—even as I worried about the sometimes-stereotypical representations—I could hear more clearly the satire and even the subtle challenges to America's racial inequality. I wouldn't have been able to articulate it then, but I was starting to feel the first faintest tugs of belonging somewhere, being a part of something bigger than myself or my suffocating little world.

Conditions with my father were growing steadily worse. I could no longer escape the stress, even at school. Sometimes I might find momentary refuge in my own imagination while working on a story in creative writing class, but otherwise I worried constantly about what I might come home to find: Would the house be in flames? Dad still smoked incessantly and often abandoned lit cigarettes in random places. He could fall asleep with one between his fingers. The danger of fire was very real to me, and ever-present. What if he turned on the stove and forgot about it? Or decided to start up the car and go for a drive? Once home, when I turned out my bedroom light at night, I never fell fully, deeply asleep.

Whatever passive concerns my extended family may have had about me on my own with Dad seemed to lessen as I grew older. Eleven going on twelve apparently signaled more resilience and resourcefulness than eight going on nine. As the space kept growing wider between visits with aunts, uncles, cousins, and my grandmother, a feeling of hopelessness grew deeper. Only Gil, though barely out of adolescence himself, remained consistent, still showing up whenever he could to take me back to Long Island for a weekend.

Gil possessed an inherent abundance of every trait for stellar success—he was handsome, gregarious, confident, fearless, and so smart, he had aced high school by the age of sixteen and was all teed up for law school. When I was four and he first went off to SUNY Stony Brook, I used to wait by the windows anxiously—sometimes for hours—for him to come home for weekend visits. I would beg him to play catch or a game, or just spend time with me. I looked up to him. But brilliance casts the darkest shadows, too, and Gil was already well on his way to embracing those counter-traits: His good looks belied an ugly temper, the confidence gave way to cockiness, his willingness to take risks fed a wild and dangerous recklessness, and his intelligence often made him more complacent than curious.

Losing his father—our mother's first husband—had been hard on him. After the divorce, Gil's father had moved to Puerto Rico to open a restaurant, and when I was little, Gil had gone to Puerto Rico each summer to spend time with his dad and work in the restaurant. The place was a popular hangout for golfers from the mainland United States who enjoyed weekending at the beautiful El Conquistador Hotel in Fajardo. Gil's dad regaled them with stories mined from his experience as a New York City taxi driver. One summer night—the way I heard my grandmother and mother talk about it—Gil's father decided to eat barracuda, consuming a fish known to be sometimes poisonous. The show of machismo intended to impress the restaurant's largely male clientele killed him. Gil's pain at losing his father so suddenly was crushing. Losing our mother not that long after put him in an alcohol-assisted tailspin.

But he was my big brother, and he seemed to love me as I did him. In seventh grade, the swaths of time he spent with me most likely saved my life.

Long Island felt a million carefree miles away from Brooklyn. A weekend at my brother's meant bowling, the arcade, cheering him and his friends on in their softball league (or more accurately, softball, beer, and pot league). We would watch the Mets, the Knicks, or the Jets, and eat dinner in restaurants. It was genuinely fun. I could let go, just be myself, and forget about the house of horrors I felt trapped in with Dad.

Going back home was always a crash landing. Dad's grip on reality was slipping faster, and there were no longer any real stretches where he seemed present. I would have welcomed even a flash of the sarcasm that used to sting me, like the time in fifth grade when I proudly presented him my "A-plus" grade on a test. I had done enough of the 20 possible extra credit points to score 116. He immediately asked me where the other 4 points were. Now our only engagements were irrational. He spent his time either in his room with the door closed or downstairs, agitated and lying in wait for me. If he was downstairs and I was lucky, I could sneak past him. The first time I held the blade of my brother's old pocketknife to my wrist was after a time I hadn't been that lucky.

After a silent dinner, Dad had started yelling at me for no reason. "What did I do to have such a lazy son?" he railed. "You're not working hard enough in school! Why aren't your grades better?" I had straight-A's, but no matter how delusional his rants were, they landed like a hunter's arrow dead-center to my heart, and I would believe every insult or disparaging remark. I was worthless. I would never amount to anything. Who did I think I was? I wasn't Keith, the brilliant grandson; or Uncle Dolly, the famous athlete; or Uncle Hal, the hero bomber pilot; or my father, the vaunted educator. I didn't have whatever magic King dust they all had. I was a pretender to that throne, a fraud. The "real" me couldn't possibly be the kid at Mark Twain who performed for teachers and classmates alike, earning A's whether I was solving an algebra problem or describing passengers in the voice of a sarcastic cabbie for creative writing class. That night in the kitchen, long past even trying to mount any argument in my own defense, I burst into shameful tears and bolted for the stairs. Dad followed, still bellowing. I ran to my room and shut the door, heading for my usual spot in front of the window, where I kept a chair to sit in while I gazed out back. The family I liked to watch wasn't in their courtyard. Our own patch of garden felt even emptier; Mom's yellow rose-bush never did rebloom after she died.

This isn't going to end, I told myself. There was no reason to think tomorrow would be any different from today, and today was unbearable.

I caught sight of the pocketknife where I kept it on the dresser and picked it up. I held the blade very close to my wrist and wondered whether I was supposed to slit horizontally or verti-cally. It was fear that made me put it down. Or maybe I simply didn't have the mental energy to figure out what direction I was supposed to cut. But I would toy with that blade against my flesh again, and again.

On top of it all, I worried that my suicidal thoughts were proof that I was "crazy" too, just like my father.

The real irony was that my father was "the rescuer" in the King family, the one who had sacrificed his own dreams of being a surgeon because medical school was too expensive, and he had to work early in life to help support his widowed mother and younger siblings.

My father had had two older brothers—Charlie and Eddie—but they had drifted into gangster life during Prohibition after their father died. One or the other was even a driver for Jack "Legs" Diamond, a notorious Irish-American bootlegger. Uncle

Hal used to love telling the story of his big brother pulling up in front of the house to see his mother, and Hal, then around five, venturing outside to gape at the big car. "Legs" got out and flipped him a quarter, which Hal—to his own joy and surprise—actually caught. I suppose he's lucky he didn't catch a juvenile racketeering charge for laundering moonshine money.

Dad, the oldest responsible sibling still at home, was less enthralled with his big brothers' career choice, and took it upon himself to make sure that the next youngest—Hal and Dolly—stayed on course and became respectable successes. He apparently was a stern taskmaster even back then, and though Dolly had died before I was born, I could see at family gatherings how Uncle Hal—a larger-than-life figure himself—deferred to Dad, still revering and perhaps even fearing him.

Raising his brothers Hal and Dolly clearly filled Dad with pride, from the stories he told, but what I experienced was that raising me, his only son, filled him with bitter anger. I knew real life wasn't like *Family Ties* or *The Cosby Show*. But theoretically at least, I knew there was something better than this—like Uncle Hal and Aunt Jean's, or the home their daughter Jan and her husband, Denauvo, had created. Cousin Jan was like a warm and wise older sister to me whenever I saw her. I knew what I had wasn't normal. That's why I didn't tell anyone.

It was June that year, just before school let out, when my grown cousin Dwight—Uncle Hal's son—came to stay for a night or two while in the city for a job interview. We were both awakened in the middle of the night by a loud thud. When I went to my father's room, Dwight was already there, helping him up off the floor. He had apparently fallen while getting up to use the bathroom. He was conscious, but a cut on his head was bleeding and looked like it needed stitches, so Dwight and I got him to the car, and we all drove to the hospital emergency room.

I was in the little curtained-off treatment bay when the doctor began asking him the kind of simple questions that I'd seen TV doctors ask: What year is this, who is the president, do you know where you are? Dad couldn't answer any, but I already knew that had nothing to do with the bump on the head. He was admitted.

Back at the house, I discovered that the bathroom he'd been trying to reach wasn't the en suite in his room; instead, he'd been relieving himself in a corner by the nightstand. He apparently had been doing so for a while. The stench was overwhelming.

Dwight had to get back home after his interview, but Uncle Hal came to stay with me. None of us knew what might happen next; Dad's condition didn't seem to be improving. School was letting out in a couple of weeks, and I couldn't begin to imagine what the summer might bring. Would he come home in a wheel-chair and need me to bathe and feed him? What about the bath-room? With Uncle Hal in the house, though, there was a certain peace and sense of normalcy. I didn't feel the constant sense of anxiety or dread. I felt safe, and relieved that someone else had assumed the responsibility—at least for now—of taking care not only of Dad, but of me, as well. Weirdly enough, that emotional rebound of sorts even carried over to getting mugged.

One sunny afternoon, two older guys—maybe eighteen or twenty—came up from behind, one of them on a bike, as I was walking home. They pushed me against the fence and the one on foot brandished a knife. They demanded money and I handed over the twenty-dollar bill I had in my wallet. The second guy jumped on the back of the bike, and they rode off. A car then squealed around the corner and came to a stop next to me as I stood there crying.

"Those guys just mug you?" a man asked me from the passenger window, flashing a police badge. "Get in!"

I jumped into the back seat and the driver spun the car around and took off in the direction the muggers had pedaled off. The police radio crackled as they called for backup en route. My twelve-year-old terror switched to an adrenaline surge of pure excitement that I was now in a chase scene right out of Hollywood (except, I guess, for the bicycle part). It was like a superhero movie—something bad had happened, but now the villains who hurt me were going to pay for it. We spotted the bike outside a bodega, the two thieves just emerging with the snacks they'd immediately spent my twenty dollars on. They were promptly arrested while I grinned with satisfaction from the back seat of my unmarked car. I was no longer a victim; I was the avenger. I was taken to the police station to give a statement, then given a ride home, where Uncle Hal was filled in on the drama.

I testified sometime later before a grand jury. It felt very serious and adult. A plea deal was struck soon after, so I never had to appear at an actual trial, but I had a very naive and satisfying first impression about the way the justice system worked. Swift and clear-cut. When you live in shifting shades of gray, always wary of what might burst forth from the shadows, the clarity of black and white is empowering. You know what to expect. Maybe part of the reason why I easily recall that incident, why I tucked it away as an anecdote about myself, is because it was so contained. It happened and was over. It was a frightening event. Not my life.

Dad was transferred to long-term care. No one explained why or what would happen next, and I went to spend the summer with Gil. Even better, Dale was invited, too. His mother, raising Dale and a younger sister on her own, agreed he could spend the summer with us on Long Island. I don't think there was any serious vetting of Gil, who knew how to crank up the charm when it was needed, but if she was thinking it might be good for Dale to have a young role model, she was sorely mistaken.

Dale and I lived it up. We spent our days playing baseball or whiffleball, going to the movies whenever we felt like it, getting Slurpees and hot dogs at 7-Eleven and eating lots of junk food, playing mini-golf, and just hanging out with Gil as our generous benefactor. What Gil did to generate income wasn't entirely clear to me—he generally had a job of sorts, bartending or maybe dabbling in real estate? As far as I know, he finished his undergrad degree, but in truth, Gil's only avid pursuit was women.

Dale and I were always welcome to tag along in his sports car when Gil hit the bars at night. He favored the kind of rowdy young hot spots where there might be pool or foosball tables, Pac-Man, or a Trivial Pursuit tournament, which Gil would always win. He had an encyclopedic knowledge of sports, and an astonishing cache of random information about pop culture, history, music, and whatever else you cared to throw at him. Gil had answers when it came to big or small questions. Life was as good as I'd ever known it.

I called my father periodically to check in on him, but he was usually out of it and responded to my questions with simple "yes" or "no," or semi-coherent ramblings. It wasn't really clear to me what was wrong with him, but I could tell he was getting worse, not better. I remember the last time I spoke to him, that August, there was just breathing, no words at all, on the other end of the line. Maybe I knew, or maybe I just hoped, that he was listening even if he couldn't answer, so I prattled on. I asked how he was doing. I told him I was having fun at Gil's and described what I had done that day. Then I said what I always did before saying goodbye.

"I love you, Daddy."

His cause of death had something to do with a catheter, though I didn't know what that meant.

Back in Brooklyn, I stayed with Uncle Hal and Aunt Jean at our house. The wake, held at the funeral home, was packed with former colleagues, friends, and people from the many civic and professional organizations my father had once belonged to. There were former students who remembered him as a teacher, professor, principal, and deputy superintendent. One man— maybe in his late fifties—came up to me and spoke reverently about what a wonderful teacher my father had been. He told me how important a role model my father was for him as a Black man, what high expectations my father had, and how he had pushed his students to do their best and to always strive for more. He hadn't talked with my father since being a student, but he saw the obituary in the paper, and knew he had to come to pay his respects to the teacher who had changed his life. His eyes welled with tears, and it was clear how much he wanted to convey his gratitude to me since he had missed the opportunity to tell my father. I offered a polite smile and merged back into the crowd.

There was a dissonance to the voices spilling quietly over and around me, all of these strangers sincerely mourning a man I never got to know. I thought I should feel sadder than I did.

I felt guilty that I wasn't crying. I couldn't reconcile the person these people were describing with the torturous period I had endured. I was resentful, too. Why hadn't I gotten to experience the inspiring teacher warmly demanding excellence from his pupils instead of the sadness, disappointment, incoherence, and rage that defined my father for me? And yet I had loved him. I did love him.

Uncle Hal and Aunt Jean asked me what I wanted to do. It struck me that I was an orphan now. They were trying to coax me to come live with them, but part of me was too angry. Everybody had left me with my father except my brother, who took me away on weekends. I knew that Hal and Gil didn't get along, but I felt a fierce loyalty toward Gil. My sister Lynne, on the other hand, was only concerned with going through the house to put stickers on everything she wanted, including things that had belonged to *my* mother, not to her father or her own late mother. When Gil saw the stickers, he was angry, but Gil was always angry on some level. The two of us went into my parents' room and took Mom's jewelry box, which looked like a miniature armoire. It still smelled like her. That was all I wanted or needed. I went back to Long Island with Gil. I chose him.

When we made a final pilgrimage to Brooklyn to collect the rest of my belongings before the new school year began, the basement had flooded, ruining boxes full of family photographs. My entire childhood, washed away.

There was a reading of my father's last will and testament, which I wasn't told about. Uncle Hal was appointed guardian. I only learned decades later, while reminiscing with Keith, that everything was left to me. That nest egg my frugal parents built up over years would stretch well into my college education.

Gil had inherited the bulk of the proceeds of my mother's life insurance and pension when she passed, and I assume that's how he secured the funds to make the down payment on a four-bedroom, two-story house with a big yard on a corner lot in a very white suburb of Long Island called Smithtown. It looked like the Brady Bunch had just moved out.

It was time to play family.

CHAPTER THREE

GIL DIDN'T THINK TWICE ABOUT LETTING ME MOVE IN WITH HIM, with what must have been Uncle Hal's wary permission. Feeling wanted fed my fantasy of getting to be just a kid for once, without having to be on constant alert for deadly emotional minefields that could explode without warning. That house on Hiawatha Lane stood as proof that my brother's intentions were selfless, his efforts heroic for a twenty-four-year-old. He was willing to change his life for me.

His lifestyle, however, was another matter. As I settled into my freshman year of high school, having skipped eighth grade courtesy of the Astor program and New York City's accelerated junior high school model, I figured Gil and I would forge our own sort of Hallmark family—two orphaned brothers making it on their own, eating burgers whenever we wanted, watching sports together, running errands in Gil's beloved Camaro. But Gil seemed intent on his bachelor routine of bar hopping, serial dating, and working only when he felt like it. No one ever doubted Gil could succeed at just about anything he set his mind to, but his preferred setting was "endless summer."

Smithtown boasted an excellent school district and appeared every bit the idyllic affluent suburb, but for a kid from Brooklyn, it was a different world. It was a weird feeling being initiated into the OBG—the Only Black Guy—club. Intuitively, I hit the "snooze" button on the racial awakening Miss D had sparked back in junior high. I was already anxious enough about being a twelve-year-old freshman with classmates already sprouting facial hair. I made a conscious choice to shift into go-along to get-along mode, my hand no longer shooting up in social studies to challenge America's painful history and ongoing reality of racial inequality. I felt like Holden Caulfield in *The Catcher in the Rye*, an adolescent observer with a continuous critique unspooling inside my head. I held that pose for two long but benign years.

The social surface I skimmed across was smooth and predictable. I had a new best friend named Bill. I envied Bill's traditional Italian Catholic family, with two loving parents, two happy, thriving boys, and everyone gathered around the table for dinner each night. It was as if I had finally managed to insinuate myself into the backyard tableau I used to view from my bedroom window in Flatlands. Bill was even on the path to Eagle Scout.

I was keen on spending time at Bill's house but didn't want him hanging out at mine. At Smithtown West High, I stage-managed a few school plays, won a couple of creative writing competitions, and maintained an A average in honors classes. Although I didn't bond with any Smithtown West teachers the way I had with Mr. Osterweil and Miss D, my classes and even my homework were a joyful refuge whether I was reading *A Tale of Two Cities* by Charles Dickens in English or *Things Fall Apart* by Chinua Achebe in social studies. I looked forward to weekend or holiday visits from my grandmother, who seemed to be counting on me—or at least my presence and the implied responsibility of me—to get Gil to settle down.

Gil was more inclined to double-down: I was forever wandering into the kitchen in the morning to see a half-dressed woman helping herself to my cereal while Gil was still sleeping off the night before. One time, he came home from the bars with a woman, her friend, and a guy the friend had picked up. They wanted water and something to eat, but the sink was full of dirty dishes, so they woke me up to wash them. Gil retreated to his bedroom with his date, leaving me at twelve years old to make awkward small talk with two extremely drunk—or possibly high—strangers.

Just after my thirteenth birthday, there was a glimmer of hope that Gil was tiring of the one-night stands when he narrowed his focus to two very different women. First, there was a sweet, earnest schoolteacher named Amy. Or maybe Amanda? Something with an "A." Amy-Amanda came from a suburban white Long Island family, either Irish or Italian, and was very family-oriented. Gil met her while bartending when Amy-Amanda was out with her friends. He got her phone number, and they went on a few dates. Anne Hathaway would play her in a rom-com.

At the same time, Gil was also pursuing Michelle, a pretty blonde who worked at a local deli. She came from an unspecified difficult childhood, had lost both parents in a car accident, and was very much on her own. Everything about her personality was edgy. She was nice enough, even faintly maternal toward me, but the word "sweet" would never be used to describe Michelle. What she exuded was aggressive, her layers complicated and hazy. Aubrey Plaza would play her in an indie thriller.

I was rooting for Amy-Amanda because I thought she would be such a stabilizing force for Gil and maybe, selfishly, for me. Normalcy was forever my Holy Grail, but Gil was not there yet. He wanted drama. He broke up with Amy-Amanda, and Michelle moved in with us soon thereafter.

Michelle came with pets—a dog and a rabbit at first. We already had Gil's cat, Buddy, and Gilly, the small turtle in a plastic pond that my brother had given me one Christmas when I was a little kid. In quick succession, we added a young black Lab called Smokey, a cat Michelle brought home, a ferret Gil wanted, then another rabbit for Michelle.

At one point, Gil's college-age cousin Edwin came from Puerto Rico to stay with us, too, and fortunately didn't bring any pets. Edwin was very nice, but he didn't have a plan, and being with Gil wasn't going to change that. With Gil and Michelle always drinking and partying and fighting, Smithtown was hardly the place for a gap year of self-reflection. Edwin soon decided to go back to Puerto Rico.

By my sophomore year at Smithtown West, Gil was getting pass-out drunk every single night, which was horrible, on the one hand, but on the other hand, I relished the guaranteed peace and predictability. Awake, Gil had no parameters for reason or risk.

One night, I remember speeding down the Long Island Expressway with him in the Camaro. It was one o'clock in the morning, and Gil was treating the LIE like the Autobahn, no speed limits to consider. The Camaro was flying when another driver cut Gil off. Gil immediately hit the accelerator even harder, swerved in front of the offender, and slammed on his brakes. I was terrified.

Both Gil and the other driver got out of their respective cars and started yelling at each other; my brother was so in the moment, there was no way to coax him back into the Camaro. Once Gil and the other guy had engaged in sufficient testosterone- and alcohol-fueled posturing, the other driver had the good sense to get back in his car and drive off.

Michelle and I were quiet partners when it came to avoiding Gil's darkest moods, but she was hardly stable herself. For start- ers, Michelle turned out to be a kleptomaniac, and a very good one at that. We would go shopping together, and she groomed me to be her accomplice with beginner-level price-tag switch- ing. Not hot-ticket items for 1988 like Swatch watches or Adi- das sneakers. Random household things, like detergent. I knew that aiding and abetting Michelle with her personal flash-sales was wrong, but life with my father had taught me the art of compartmentalizing before I was even ten. As with school, I just kept going along to get along and threw in a few prayers that store security didn't catch us. I would talk with Uncle Hal on the phone periodically and visit Cherry Hill for family gath- erings in the summer, but the Kings never visited me at Gil's house, and I felt too defensive—both of my brother and my own misguided choice to live with him—to admit what life in Smithtown was really like.

It didn't take long for Gil and me to both start noticing how Michelle's stories and purported history changed frequently, sometimes by a bit, sometimes by a mile. Suspiciously, she also kept getting mail bearing different variations of her name or other names altogether addressed to Hiawatha Lane. Domesticity wasn't Michelle's—or any of her aliases'—thing, but still, I sometimes felt her genuine concern for me, like when she would make sure I was eating, even taking it upon herself to cook an occasional meal. Mostly we lived off deli or bar food, carryout, cheap restaurants, and basic groceries.

The drunken battles between Gil and Michelle were constant and growing more intense the longer they were together. Each would try to enlist me in their conflict. Michelle and I were allies trying to navigate Gil's drinking and moods, but then Gil would complain to me about Michelle being "bitchy," as he put it, not to mention a pathological liar.

Sometimes they shoved each other, or he would say something mean and she would go to slap him, and he'd grab her—either one might initiate it, but Gil was so much bigger than Michelle, and the threat of injury was always there for her. One night, she began punching him and Gil was pushing back hard, with me as the horrified bystander. Even after that skirmish subsided, I couldn't shake off the feeling that disaster was looming, like one of those massive earthquakes where those lucky enough to escape are then buried alive by the even-worse aftershocks.

Gil and Michelle would break up, she'd leave, then she'd come back, then the cycle would repeat. They lived inside their fights, feeding off the vitriol, oblivious to the world around them. The dysfunction just kept intensifying, eating away at the thin veneer of normalcy I'd staked my future on. I fell into a depressingly familiar routine: forging checks now with my brother's name to keep the lights on, washing piles of crusted dishes so we would have plates to eat off, doing laundry for all three of us with our misbegotten Tide. In no time at all, I had become the sole caregiver for two alcoholics, two dogs, two cats, two rabbits, a ferret, and a turtle. But this time, something was different: I knew I deserved better.

The affirmation of Mr. Osterweil and Miss D had taken hold. *I can't do this again*, I told myself. I was fourteen years old, done managing the adults in my life. And this time, I had an escape plan.

My old friend from Mr. Osterweil's class, Dale, had gone away to prep school in Massachusetts on a full scholarship. His descriptions of the blissful, scholarly life at Groton piqued my interest, and I began researching elite boarding schools, ultimately setting my sights on Phillips Academy Andover.

The campus looked beautiful in the brochures, and the school's reputation for academic rigor made it a proven pathway to the Ivy League for top students. My cousin Jan's husband, Denauvo, offered his expertise as an educator and helped me with the application. I don't remember even wondering where the money for tuition and costs might come from. I just had to get in. (I don't know to this day exactly how much my parents left me, but until I reached adulthood, Uncle Hal always ensured my needs were met.)

I knew that going to live with Uncle Hal and Aunt Jean was still an option, but I also knew that, in Gil's mind, that would be the worst kind of betrayal. Gil's resentment of my father— his hated stepfather—carried over to all of the Kings. Andover was my compromise exit strategy. I mentioned nothing to Gil until I got my acceptance letter and boarding school was a done deal. I still felt guilty leaving my brother after all he had done for me—or tried to—and I dreaded telling him. I knew Gil would be livid, and think I was ungrateful, but I couldn't ignore the survival instinct urging me to go, get out, get out now.

"I bought this house for *you!*" he exploded when I finally confessed. We were family, Gil angrily reminded me, and family didn't abandon family. The words stung: a passive-aggressive jab at all the King relatives who'd left me on my own with my father. It only made matters worse for Gil that Uncle Hal and Aunt Jean were waiting to take me to Cherry Hill to live with them for the summer before dropping me off at Andover in the fall. In Gil's mind, I had defected to the enemy's camp.

After I drove off with Hal and Jean, it was months before my brother would even speak to me again. I was relieved when he did. I needed to leave him, but I didn't want to lose him.

Hal and Jean's house brimmed with its own very different kind of chaos, the happy noise of cousins coming and going, dripping water from the pool onto Aunt Jean's clean floors, neighbors and friends popping in just to say hello and staying past midnight.

Aunt Jean ran a tight ship with an abundance of love. She could discipline and dote on you simultaneously. Dinner was at the same time every night—a hot, home-cooked meal with everyone at the table passing food, joking, rehashing their days, while Uncle Hal held court. He and my father were similar that way.

Every day, I would hop on my bike and cruise around the neighborhood or jump in the pool with cousins and friends— there were always games of Marco Polo or cannonball contests underway. I felt carefree for the first time since my mom died. Uncle Hal would invite me along to run errands with him to the bank, butcher, or grocery store—and I would soak up his man-to-man advice along the way. His Tuskegee valor was still unacknowledged by the country he served, but Uncle Hal was forever the consummate soldier. Life was about serving the greater good, not seeking the greater glory. Everything in Uncle Hal and Aunt Jean's realm felt so calm and steady. *This is normal,* I concluded.

By the time the school year was ready to begin, I was secretly second-guessing my choice to leave. I didn't really want to go to Andover anymore now that escape wasn't imperative. I could stay in Cherry Hill forever. It felt too late to change my mind, though, so I packed my bags and headed to New England, faking excitement as best I could.

CHAPTER FOUR

IN THE TINY TOWN SURROUNDING THE ANDOVER CAMPUS, THE crisp white Memorial Bell Tower atop Samuel Phillips Hall is visible a mile away, 117 feet tall with a 37-bell carillon that chimes in honor of alumni who lost their lives in World War I. The school grounds encompass over 65 acres of woodlands and ponds. In spring, the surviving cherry trees from Japan's initial gift of over 100 saplings burst into frilly white and pink bloom. Each autumn, all the maples and elms flame scarlet and gold. "Idyllic" barely does the campus justice. Everyone was polite, friendly, and well scrubbed.

School administrators had insisted I was too young to be an eleventh grader, but I didn't mind being a sophomore again—the classes were all new to me, and I was looking forward to the curriculum. The rule book was tedious and prim—the worst offense, it seemed, was violating something called "parietals." I had never encountered the word before. It sounded medical, and the Oxford Dictionary would confirm that hunch, describing bones in the skull.

At Andover, parietals referred to having a member of the opposite sex in your dorm room—this particular application of the word drawing on the Latin word for "walls." Parietals posed no immediate problem: I would be sharing my dorm room with a boy from Memphis named Cardell Orrin, and we instantly hit it off. Neither of us even knew where the girls' dorms were...yet.

That first night, I unpacked my belongings and neatly arranged them, then went to dinner in a formal dining hall filled with imposing wooden tables reminiscent of every movie you've seen set at an elite New England boarding school. Then I returned to my dorm room, climbed into my narrow bed, and quietly cried myself to sleep, certain that I had just made the biggest mistake of my life.

I wasn't wrong.

Maybe it was because I was fourteen, or because I had already experienced so much trauma and nobody did anything about it, or most likely, it was all of this, but I was mad from the moment I arrived at Andover. The campus was certifiably beautiful, the teachers talented and devoted, the list of fun, interesting activities available to students long and enticing. But I was deeply, deeply angry and keen to pick fights with authority. I even turned one of my favorite subjects, AP European history, into a battleground, sparring with the teacher in a way that was entirely new to me.

The field trips we took in Mr. Osterweil's class and the meaty discussions later on in Miss D's had laid the foundation for a deep love of social studies and its myriad themes—from Renaissance art to colonialism. In some ways, Andover's class was like filling in the other side of a story I had already read: Instead of learning about the first encounters between the Aztecs and Incas with European explorers, we were learning about the European context for the so-called "Age of Exploration." This time, the story came not only without questioning or critique, but with what felt to my increasingly activist ears like a whitewashing.

I interpreted the lack of discussion or debate as an unwillingness to challenge the morality of stealing the land, wealth, and even human beings from another society. The tipping point came when the teacher, Mr. Smith—a track coach with a patrician bearing and some seniority on the history faculty—decided to take a small detour during a lesson about Cecil Rhodes. How lucky any of us might be one day, he remarked, to earn a Rhodes Scholarship, to have the privilege of studying at Oxford. To join the esteemed ranks of Nobel and Pulitzer Prize winners, people like scientist Edwin Hubble, the Knicks star and later New Jersey Senator Bill Bradley, or then–Arkansas Governor Bill Clinton. Mr. Smith was still rattling off the names of great Rhodes Scholars in history when I piped in and said with all the outrage I could muster: "I wouldn't want a scholarship that bears the name of a colonizer who made his name and his wealth exploiting Black people." Once he got over his surprise at my hostile tone, Mr. Smith called my objections "naive" and "ridiculous."

It was my turn to be stunned. His ridicule was the polar opposite of what I had encountered with Mr. Osterweil and Miss D, and their practice of taking students' perspectives seriously and engaging with our arguments earnestly, treating us as worthy of respect no matter how young or naive we might have been. The point was always to engage, never to defeat, let alone dismiss. Mr. Smith and I went back and forth a few times, me increasingly indignant bordering on disrespectful, him trying to reassert control of the classroom and perhaps by extension the social order. Eventually, he moved on, but something shifted for me: I knew I wasn't going to just keep my head down and stay quiet anymore on issues of race and social justice the way I had at Smithtown West.

Students of color were scarce at Andover in the late 1980s and early 1990s—a population small enough that you were always conscious of your otherness (at least I was). I joined Af-Lat-Am, the Black and Latino student association, and began wearing a then-popular Black Power symbol—a green, yellow, and red rendering of the African continent embossed on a black leather medallion dangling from a braided cord around my neck. The bulk of Black and Latino students came from city schools and were on scholarship. Only a handful were from wealthier families; they seemed likeliest to have white friends. I fell somewhere in between, urban by way of growing up in Brooklyn and going to New York City public schools, but upper-middle-class and semi-suburban by way of my parents' education and living in Smithtown and Cherry Hill. My urban Black peers possessed far more social awareness than I did, but ironically, I could identify with a good number of the rich white kids, by way of family dysfunction. The trust fund babies and I tended to share abandonment issues we never talked about. Plenty of them had raised themselves, too, dispatched to boarding schools as early as grade school, virtually abandoned by parents too busy jet-setting or running business empires or managing their social calendars to be bothered raising them or even seeing them outside specified holidays at ski resorts or tropical islands. Andover operated as "in loco parentis"—in the actual absence of parents. At the end of the day, though, it was anything but. And at the end of the day,

John B. King Jr.

it wasn't Andover's rules, structure, order or expectations that I rebelled against—those were the very things I had yearned for in my father's house, and then my brother's. Chaos scared me and anarchy burdened me. I wanted the kind of authority Uncle Hal exuded—a wise, firm, but ultimately loving hand. Rules were never my undoing. But at Andover, rules in the absence of love were about to be.

One of the first things I noticed about my new "Phillips family" was how white students and students of color generally sat separately at mealtime, with the exception of some predominantly white tables with a smattering of non-white classmates. There were only forty or fifty of us fully engaged Af-Lat-Am activists at most, our numbers small enough to form a tight-knit clan. It wasn't so much that we felt distinctly unwelcome at the "white tables"—it was that we didn't have to feel uncertain or guarded among ourselves at our own table surrounded by friends who were going through the exact same things. Especially for new students at Phillips Academy, the camaraderie provided a safe shore, a place to gather confidence and courage before setting sail. Those mealtimes at the Black and Latino students' tables also gave me a chance to fill in the cultural gaps from those years of isolation when caring for my father: I listened keenly for the cult-classic one-liners from movies I'd never seen, or the backstories of some musician or performer I didn't know, or slang words I hadn't heard. I had a lot of catching up to do, to belong to my own generation.

My own 1990 musical taste ran to A Tribe Called Quest or Public Enemy or my favorite, Keith Sweat, one of the godfathers of R & B, who had a video featuring a sad clown playing the saxophone for a jilted guy brooding in a paisley smoking jacket.

My classmates blasted the edgier N.W.A. or Too Short from their radios and watched MTV videos with hot dancers (who did not wear smoking jackets).

The racial dynamic on campus played out in extracurriculars as well. Overt ostracism wasn't the problem as much as a blanket disinterest in and dismissal of the lives of the non-white prep school students. It was mostly students of color who turned out for the step shows or slam poetry nights organized by Af-Lat-Am.

Af-Lat-Am was an eclectic group—you were as likely to find the scholarship son of migrants who worked the strawberry fields in California as the wealthy daughter of a jailed Nigerian president overthrown in a coup. Our diversity united instead of divided us, flipping the norm of the "real world" inside out.

The club fed me emotionally, and the unconditional support emboldened me from the moment I'd first set foot in a meeting.

The school library was, of course, at the top of my list for exploring the campus after I unpacked. I was eager to peruse the shelves and continue the literary quest for racial identity Miss D and my brother's old bookshelf had sparked in me. Instead, I was puzzled by how few books by Black and Latino authors were displayed—let alone highlighted—on Andover's shelves. I recognized some of the classics I had already read, but I had somehow expected to find a bigger and more thoughtful collection, maybe some emerging writers to discover.

I began looking up Black and Latino authors in the card catalogs, taking careful note of how few copies Andover had of their books. The most robust collection about Black people focused on Ebonics, which struck me as weirdly outdated and borderline offensive at the least. I wondered who had decided to make that investment and why. My indignation led me to shed my quiet-observer persona and speak up at an Af-Lat-Am meeting, where I described my research, presented my findings, and—a first for me—suggested we do something about the problem. Merely winning debates on some issue wasn't going to cut it for me anymore; I hungered for action, change. Maybe Mr. Smith's dismissiveness had served a purpose, rerouting my overarching anger into passion and direction.

Everybody began excitedly bouncing around ideas about how to make our voices heard: Circulate a petition? Organize a student protest? In that moment of shared frustration and adolescent urgency and exchange, I suddenly felt overcome by a deep sense of community. If I were to choose a moment where I became an activist, that would have to be it.

I ended up drafting a paper outlining my findings and our concerns, and the club politely asked to meet with the library director. Which went nowhere.

In the end, Andover announced some vague policy change along the lines of promising to take this under advisement in the future, but there was no satisfying moment of victory in our fevered battle. Far from feeling defeated by the library skirmish, though, I actually felt empowered. There was something fulfilling about organizing around an issue and giving it voice and trying to make it better. For the time being, I was willing to accept possibility alone as victory.

With the sour taste from AP world history and Cecil Rhodes lingering in my self-righteous mouth, I went on to find new spaces outside the classroom for my revived interest in race and socioeconomic inequities, signing up for the Political Economy Club—an informal political debating club that echoed TV's *The McLaughlin Group* in form and substance. *The McLaughlin*

Group—famously parodied on *Saturday Night Live*—was named for the popular TV personality and political commentator, John McLaughlin, who had been a speechwriter for President Richard Nixon. He would gather a group of pundits—a couple on the left (like Clarence Page or Eleanor Clift) and a couple on the right (like Fred Barnes or Pat Buchanan) and then throw out political questions for them to debate. Sometimes the insights were fascinating; other times they just seemed to be yelling at each other. Questionable role models aside, the Political Economy Club provided an outlet for super-nerdy teens who felt the need to talk through public policy, and I was grateful for that much. Leaving my middle school dalliance with Reaganism far in the rearview mirror, I was more than happy to join a campus pro-choice protest when President Bush visited. The Bush legacy at Andover ran deep: President George H. W. Bush had graduated in 1942, and regularly returned for alumni and trustee meetings or special events even into his nineties. He loved Andover so much that he sent all three of his sons there, too. Before becoming president himself, George W. Bush, class of '64, honed his leadership skills as a baseball player and head cheerleader at Andover.

Genteel and diverse as Andover appeared to be in the brochures, racial tensions were always at a decibel 10 on campus. Every semester, there would be some racial incident—a problematic cartoon in the campus paper or controversy over a speaker or event. The overall tone toward Black and Latino students repeatedly felt condescending, like Andover was doing us a favor by letting us attend. The school often manifested white privilege and elitism. Students of color were supposed to be grateful to be there, and I was not. I didn't hold up my end of the bargain. I came to escape a bad situation, not because I truly wanted what Andover offered.

As difficult as it was to be a student of color at Andover in the '80s and '90s, the handful of teachers of color offered another version of the school where we could thrive and succeed. My portal to that alter-academy was Edith Walker, my calculus teacher, who told me when we met that her mother had been a student of my father's early on in his career. Ms. Walker tutored me after class. She served as a resident dorm mother and had an apartment in one of the girls' dormitories. Ms. Walker was African-American but had very light skin, and white people often assumed she was white. But she had grown up in a Black family and in a Black context, and she was very clear about her own identity. Even after I got my math skills on track, I liked to go for tutoring just to talk. She shared stories about some of her early experiences and unease at Andover, when she would overhear white teachers at faculty social gatherings talk about students of color as not being up to snuff academically. Saying they didn't belong at Andover. It was only after they began to notice that Ms. Walker socialized with faculty members of color and talked about Af-Lat-Am activities or events she was attending, like step (dance) shows, that racist gossip fell quiet when she was in earshot.

There was nothing to do in the sleepy little town of Andover itself, but sometimes on weekends, Cardell and I would head into Cambridge to get our hair cut at a Black barbershop. I loved the urban energy and ethnic diversity of Cambridge with its street musicians, coffee shops, and the bustling sidewalks full of Harvard students. I had never been to a Black barbershop before Cardell took me. There's no single word to fully capture what I felt sitting there, waiting my turn, listening to Black men all banter about sports, music, women, and movies. The conversation was free flowing, and anyone was welcome to chime in or dip out whenever they pleased. I felt very adult, and I loved that these barbers didn't seem perplexed by my hair when I sat down. I didn't just feel like I belonged there; I felt as if I had always been there. I didn't have to fit in, be accepted, or tolerated. I didn't have to impress, amaze, or be over-welcomed with effusive attention. I wasn't an exception to unspoken rules or traditions, or proof that any person or institution was "progressive." I could just be. Holden Caulfield retreated, and I stepped into the space he had left behind.

The summer after that first year at Andover, I ended up in Maryland, living with my cousin Jan and her husband, Denauvo. Uncle Hal and Aunt Jean often spent long stretches of their summers on cruise ships, heading to some exotic or interesting place. Jan and Denauvo were a happy fill-in for home base. I had spent more time with Jan than I had with my own two half sisters, and I instantly felt part of her small family in Randallstown.

She and Denauvo had a little boy, Deviré, who was five years old. Denauvo was the kind of father I wished I had: engaged, strict but playful, beaming with pride over Deviré. Jan and Denauvo both took clear delight in watching their son learn. Denauvo made it his mission that summer to teach me to stop carrying the world on my fifteen-year-old shoulders. We'd have marathon games of Monopoly and laugh the entire time, play-wrestle with Deviré, or just toss a ball back and forth in the soft summer twilight before supper.

I found myself drawn into the complicated world of Denauvo's students at the school where he served as headmaster in one of Baltimore's most impoverished, violent communities. Their struggles with difficult home environments felt familiar, even if the gangs and shootings they experienced in their neighborhood did not. Denauvo's devotion to them and absolute conviction that his school could give them a path to a better future inspired me. When he would tell their stories, much like my mother describing her students at Bildersee, I was rooting desperately for hopeful endings.

I had a job that summer, too, as a bookkeeper at the accounting firm Bennett, Hutt & Co. It was a modest office that Louis Hutt had founded at the age of twenty-eight. Later, his younger brother and all three of his children would end up joining the family business. The firm's declared mission was to treat clients as if they were family, and Louis Hutt did just that. He was only thirty-seven when I worked there, but he exuded an almost grandfatherly warmth and wisdom. I watched and eavesdropped all summer in the mom-and-pop office as clients parked themselves at his desk. Louis would, without fail, lean forward, look them in the eye, and ask, "How *you* doin'?" and mean it. Really mean it. He engaged every single person who came through his door, listening earnestly whether they were trying to figure out their finances or their lives. He gave an independent contractor working construction the same attention as a restaurant owner with ten franchises.

It was easy to see my Uncle Hal as a leader, given his military background, but Mr. Hutt made me see good leadership through a prism other than awards, honors, titles, certificates, or degrees (all of which Louis Hutt had framed on a full wall). He was a confident administrator and expert at tax advice, but I could see what really made him effective were his relationships, not merely his expertise. Louis never feigned interest in his clients; he actually did want to hear about their arthritis or wedding plans or landlord troubles, not because it mattered to him, but because it mattered to them. "How can I be of service to you?" wasn't an empty greeting. His light was the energy that powered the firm.

When Denauvo returned me to Andover that fall, I had mixed feelings about going back. I had a new roommate—a white guy from South Carolina named Jason Dennis—and a different dorm. Jason and I shared an interest in politics, which had broken the ice and led to our friendship, and I was happy to reunite with Cardell and my Af-Lat-Am friends. What really stopped me from asking Denauvo to come get me, though, was the prospect of having Mr. Rogers for US history.

Mr. Rogers was hugely popular with the students, famous for his keen sense of humor, and he confronted race relations head-on. His gift for storytelling made his classes seem more like performances than lectures. He reminded me a lot of Miss D that way. One of the few Black faculty members, he drilled deeply into topics like the civil rights movement, the nineteenth-century labor movement, or early progressive efforts to combat and overcome inequality in America. He invited open discussion and spurred us on to explore and thoroughly examine our points of view rather than merely express them. In a time where Robin Williams and Edward James Olmos were crushing the box office with *Dead Poets Society* and *Stand and Deliver*, respectively, playing charismatic teachers deeply engaging their students, Mr. Rogers was the real thing. In his class, saying what you thought was just the starting point. Mr. Rogers also wanted to know where that thought was taking you.

I gradually assimilated into life at Andover, but I knew I was still hiding in plain sight. I never shared my family story with my classmates, and nobody gave my reserve a second thought. Many of the kids of color had working-class parents who couldn't take time off or afford to come visit on weekends or for special events, so the absence of mine didn't make me stand out. The rich white parents were just as likely to be no-shows. Many of them had sent their kids off to boarding school to be rid of the mundane details of their everyday school lives. But when I started eleventh grade, I did start to stand out from the crowd for other reasons. Or one reason. Her name was Grace. Grace was in my class but also beyond it. Tenth graders were considered "lowers" at Andover, and Grace was dating a popular twelfth grader. He was practically in college. The two of them glided through campus life like royalty, the kind of power couple destined for yearbook greatness.

When Cardell and I used to talk in our dorm room as we were getting ready to go to sleep about our "ideal girl," I would bring up Grace the same way some people would go on about Lisa Bonet or Janet Jackson. Not just out of my league, but out of my—and most everyone else's—galaxy. Grace was smart, beautiful, and popular. She came from Little Rock, Arkansas, the daughter of an African-American mother and Nigerian father. We became friends through Af-Lat-Am, but after her boyfriend graduated, our banter turned to flirtation. In eleventh grade, as newly uppers, we became an item. Basking in royalty by osmosis, I had arrived.

We broke parietals with abandon, and I quickly learned about the secret brick the cool kids in my dorm used to keep the side door wedged open so you could slip back in after curfew. I was immature and a bit rudderless, still struggling to figure out who I was, but I was also not quite sixteen and thus invincible. I was far too clever to even consider the possibility of getting caught. Then came the night when Becky Sykes, the cluster dean, magnanimously took a shift for the usual resident assistant. Mrs. Sykes was waiting in the stairwell when I slipped back in like the Pink Panther.

"Where have you been?" she demanded. I quickly replied that my cousin came to town unexpectedly and had taken me out to dinner in Boston. Mrs. Sykes asked for his phone number, and I claimed I couldn't remember it. Or the name of the restaurant. Mrs. Sykes didn't flat out accuse me of lying but said I needed evidence.

I went to see her the next day, hoping to plead my case. Becky Sykes and her husband, Elwin, were the closest thing to a faculty version of couple royalty. The Sykeses and their three sons were one of the few Black families on campus, prominent members of the campus community. Elwin Sykes was a beloved English teacher, while his wife was a career administrator. They'd met during high school in segregated Louisiana and married while at Harvard. Mrs. Sykes was a trim, smartly dressed woman whose slight, lilting Southern drawl belied a no-nonsense resolve. We sat in the kitchen of her campus apartment, and for the first time, I shared my life story. It sounded more like a recitation of facts— the premise to some tragic debate—than a plea for mercy. I had never recounted it all out loud like that. I knew on some level that my traumatic, lost childhood had more to do with my anger and lack of respect for adults than Andover and its parietals did, but other than the anger, I simply had no way yet to express that. Mrs. Sykes listened to me dispassionately, and all I could do was hope that the school would give me another chance. I couldn't even say with any conviction that I loved Andover and belonged there. My desperation was born of aspiration, not emotion. How else would I get to Harvard?

I ended up having to go before the discipline board, where I admitted lying, but I still refused to say where I had actually been or with whom. I didn't want to get anyone else in trouble. I was put on probation.

Far from being scared straight, I added truancy to my burgeoning rebel portfolio.

I hated my AP chemistry class, unable to connect with either subject or teacher. The daily lectures were dry and humorless. When I seemed distracted in class, there was no encouragement like Miss D's; when I struggled with the homework and tests, there was no invitation to come to tutoring like Ms. Walker's. I started skipping on a regular basis. There's basically no way to do that *without* getting caught. I was warned, and then I would do it again. Eventually the school and I both decided I might be better off in regular chemistry instead of the advanced class, which resolved the habitual truancy over compounds and substrates, but it didn't stop me from skipping other classes.

There were days when I just wouldn't do anything except sleep or stay in my dorm room. I also stopped showing up for my assigned rotation for dorm chores, like cleaning bathrooms or common areas. I just couldn't muster any energy or motivation. It's easy as an adult to see that I was seriously depressed, but if any adult at Andover suspected as much, they never said or did anything. I simply didn't fit Andover's usual infrastructure of problem kids—drinking or doing drugs or flunking classes—and they were unsure what to do about me.

From their perspective, I was a "minority kid" who was doing well academically while refusing to turn in certain assignments or follow rules.

My relationship with Grace suffered as well. We were always tumultuous in that intensely dramatic way adolescent love inevitably is, but we eventually broke up because I wasn't a consistently attentive and supportive boyfriend. I was moody, working through my own issues and unable to explain myself to anyone. The school naturally alerted my guardian about my disciplinary issues, and Uncle Hal sternly warned me that he would pull me out if I didn't straighten up. Even that didn't faze me.

In the spring semester, my AP comparative government teacher told the class we could choose between writing a paper or taking a final exam. I opted for the paper. I didn't write a word, and missed the deadline for turning it in. Then I sauntered into the exam as if I had chosen that option all along. I ended up getting an A in the class but "with unsatisfactory effort." At Andover, the latter was worse than a failing grade. It meant you had failed them.

I knew I was on thin ice now.

On the last day of exams, I was on my way to my math final when I realized I had forgotten a pencil. I was walking back to my dorm to get one when I ran into a girl I knew, and she walked with me. Neither of us was thinking about parietals when she followed me into my room. We were stopped by a dorm monitor on our way out. I had just violated probation. And now, because of a forgotten pencil, I could be expelled. This time, there wouldn't be any appearance before the board. The faculty would review my folder and vote on my fate after the students left for the summer. I returned to New Jersey unsure whether I would be back that September.

Uncle Hal answered the phone when Becky Sykes called to say Andover was expelling me. He held the phone with cold steel in his expression, and I could tell he was furious.

After he hung up, it turned out Uncle Hal's anger was directed at Becky Sykes and Andover, not me. He was angry at "them," the nameless, faceless people and the entrenched enmity of an unequal and unjust system of punishment and rewards in America. He was well aware that I had gotten too cocky and was screwing up at Andover. He knew that I had broken school rules, crossed some lines. But a lifetime of exceeding the system's expectations and being slapped down for it had given Lieutenant Colonel Haldane King a different perspective of those lines than I had at sixteen.

Given how strongly he felt, it's a credit to his integrity that Uncle Hal chose to relay Andover's offer to reenroll me after a year away at another school, just so I could graduate from Phillips Academy.

Since Andover had already made me repeat tenth grade when I initially enrolled solely because of my age, this offer meant I would have six years of high school.

Defeat shifted instantly to jubilation. I immediately leaped at the chance, hugely relieved that Andover was offering to take me back. I was angry at myself for having sabotaged my own future. I could undo the mess I had made! My academic future was salvageable! Of course I would repeat my senior year!

Then I noticed that Uncle Hal's flinty expression hadn't changed. "No," he said. "You're not going back." I would enroll at Cherry Hill West High School that fall and earn my diploma there.

I was outraged. Why was he butting into my business? Why should he get to decide? He hadn't stepped in when life with my father was torturing me. It wasn't fair for him to take this second chance away from me. He knew I had dreams of going to Princeton or Harvard—the Ivy League wasn't going to touch me with an expulsion on my record. Back and forth we argued, but no matter how logical or impassioned a point I made, Uncle Hal refused to budge. And as my legal guardian, he held all the power.

"Neither you nor I can change things that happened to you," he calmly said, "but you have to decide what kind of life you want to have, what kind of man you want to be."

He didn't have to speak the underlying message out loud: If I wanted to get to Princeton, Harvard—or anywhere else in the world—I needed to arrive under my own power, not anyone else's.

He didn't have to explain himself further, because Uncle Hal had embodied this principle and fought to uphold it his entire life. It's why everyone who knew Haldane King—me included—admired him so deeply.

Uncle Hal enlisted in the military at the age of twenty-one, soon after the United States became engaged in World War II. He left his home in Brooklyn to report to Alabama for basic training during a time when Jim Crow laws were still upheld in many states and segregation in the military and the federal government prevailed. Tuskegee Institute had been contracted by the US Army Air Corps to help train the country's first Black military aviators. The university already boasted a highly successful civilian pilot-training program but turned its attention toward the war effort to prepare Uncle Hal and 921 other young

Black men for air combat, every one of them willing to put his life on the line for a country that still regularly denied Black people equal rights. Hal was in the first class of Tuskegee bomber pilots.

In Alabama, Uncle Hal learned to navigate a segregated Southern town where racism seeped into every moment of life for his all-Black squadron. Whether they were barred from the officers' club and had to eat sandwiches in the hangar or their cockpits during layovers or were forced to check the fuel tanks of their aircraft before takeoff to ensure that white soldiers hadn't tampered with them, the service had taught Uncle Hal all he needed to know about being a Black man in America.

Returning from World War II, his service and bravery unacknowledged because of his skin color, Hal couldn't even apply for a job as a pilot for the handful of commercial airlines because they all banned "Negroes" from the cockpit. Glamorous jobs like pilot were white jobs; luggage porter was the kind of job Black men returning from war could expect to get, no matter how many flights they had flown through enemy fire and safely landed.

Hal became an accountant, but that field was likewise off-limits because no firm wanted to trust a "Negro" with finances. He kept going and answered a recruitment ad to become one of New York City's first African-American firefighters. He was hired and joined an engine company, only to be shunned by the white "brotherhood" of the firehouse. He ended up being recalled by the newly integrated Air Force during the Korean War to serve and protect even those who would demean him.

Haldane King spent nineteen more years in the military before retiring at the Pentagon. He then worked his way up the corporate ladder in private industry to eventually run the same Philadelphia hospital where his own mother had worked as a nurse before he was born, and then became deputy executive director of the Delaware River Port Authority. Time and time again, Uncle Hal had answered prejudice with perseverance, forging over the course of his lifetime not one but several different careers, always challenging himself to explore unfamiliar roads and unexpected detours until they, too, were mastered. Now he was giving me no choice but to embark on a rockier road than I had planned, forcing me to trust that clarity of purpose would carry me where I was meant to go.

Staying in Cherry Hill that year put me in a different place mentally and physically. In his retirement, Uncle Hal was working for an experimental state program that offered parole for select inmates who agreed to a program of intense supervision. They could earn their freedom through this second chance by staying sober and submitting to regular drug testing while pursuing an education or keeping a job. They had to comply with a strict curfew and meet other benchmarks. Uncle Hal had designed a similar program for his teen nieces and nephews or other young family members he and Aunt Jean took in after they'd fallen off track. It was referred to only half jokingly as Uncle Hal's Reclamation Project for troubled cousins. Now I was one of them.

The balance of structure, independence, and love that Uncle Hal and Aunt Jean provided stilled the anger that had been building for so long inside me, and the depression lifted. It felt like I got to just *be* for a year. I had my own TV family at last. When Jan and Deviré joined us, while Denauvo was away in Louisiana working on his PhD at Grambling, it just added to the sense of family. The peace of just knowing that tomorrow was going to be like today, that I could count on being loved and cared for, gave me the space I needed to recalibrate. I settled into Cherry Hill West comfortably, made friends, and did well. It was my third high school. Weirdly, royal blue was each school's color. Even weirder, Cherry Hill West clung to a motto that was a throwback from its founding refrain of 1956: "Respect, Responsibility and American Citizenship."

When a student ambassador from Harvard who happened to be Black visited Cherry Hill West one day to talk to potential recruits, I was among the students invited to the meet-and-greet the guidance counselors arranged. Academically, there was no doubt in my mind that Harvard was the pinnacle of excellence, but our visitor's depiction of a vibrant, multicultural campus got me fantasizing about the kind of life I might have there.

By the time I sat down with my counselor, Mrs. Johnson, to talk about college applications, I had fallen back to earth. My record would show that I was expelled from Andover, a big mark against me no matter how high my GPA or how impressive my test scores.

Mrs. Johnson could see that I was deflated and anxious. She pulled out my folder and began reciting the AP classes I had taken, the top grades I had earned, the extracurriculars I had been involved in. I would have to write a supplemental essay explaining everything if I applied to Harvard, but I was in control of my story, Mrs. Johnson affirmed, not Andover.

This was my chance not to merely recount what happened, but why. I could provide perspective, prove that I was more than the sum of my mistakes. Argue my own case: I thrived in the classroom no matter how bleak the situation was at home, and thanks to teachers who believed in me, my passion to learn had never faltered. Mrs. Johnson gave me a hug before sending me back to class. I ended up applying to eight schools, including Georgetown, Morehouse, Stanford, Princeton, and Harvard, my first choice. *If*, I thought to myself, *I can get into any of them at all.*

The fat acceptance packets came one after the other until finally the mailbox yielded the envelope I was waiting for, bearing the logo of a crimson shield and an open book with gold letters spelling out the word *veritas.* Latin for truth.

Harvard was welcoming me to the Class of '96.

CHAPTER FIVE

Glitter pens. Did I have enough?

This wasn't the kind of question I had expected to ponder at Harvard, but I also hadn't figured on running a mini-Staples from the living room of my very first apartment. Still, there I was an adult at last. Eighteen years old with full agency over my own life and livelihood, free to follow any dream, act on any impulse, or embark on any adventure that beckoned. The move to Mission Hill deserves a category of its own, since the apartment I elected to call home the summer after my freshman year happened to be in the middle of one of Boston's most troubled public housing projects. And because of that particular choice, the summer of 1993 was about to transform me in ways that couldn't be anticipated or adequately explained, only lived.

Freshman year had presented its ups and downs. I went from the initial exhilaration of walking through the ancient gates that open into Harvard Yard thinking, *Now my life begins*, to demoralizing bouts of imposter syndrome every time I entered a packed lecture hall or passed a knot of seemingly carefree peers heading to their next class. Buying the T-shirt or hoodie with the prestigious crimson emblem didn't cement my identity as a Harvard man. *Who was I fooling? Myself? The Admissions Office? The world?* For the first time in my academic life, I felt my confidence falter.

While I had struggled mightily with life at Andover, the academics were always the best part. My Harvard class contained the lowest number of incoming Black freshmen in twenty years. I had always been a serious student, but now I doubled down and worked even harder, intimidated by the achievements, knowledge, and silent assessments of my classmates. Everyone seemed to have been a superstar at their high school, and in my imagination at least, I was the only one who didn't feel assured that my usual spot was waiting for me in that familiar A-plus stratosphere. I instantly fell into my default setting where I'd observe and listen to make myself small so no one would notice I didn't belong there. I made my way through dormitory halls moving like a shadow among the raucous laughter and camaraderie of students who were just like me, and nothing like me. On my very first day, I heard someone playing guitar down the hall outside one of the rooms. There was Jason Cooper, my "archrival" from Mr. Osterweil's class, surrounded by a group of new friends. Of course it was. It came as no surprise to learn that Jason was intent on becoming an entertainment lawyer. He practically had a corner office reserved. My plan was to concentrate (Harvard's word for your choice of major) in government, but I hadn't locked in on any specific path to my future yet. I was only seventeen, but already I could hear the clock ticking on my future career.

As the leaves began to turn and the air grew crisp, I became acutely aware that I lacked a community of peers I could consider my people. I was making friends but didn't have a group I felt super close to. I had more chats than real conversations. At the freshman dining hall, I struggled to figure out where to sit. There were people I knew from classes or my dorm, but none of them were friends I could let down my guard with. I yearned for a space like the Af-Lat-Am table at Andover, where everyone could just forget collective angst for forty-five minutes to be unabashedly themselves. One evening, after yet another dinner of polite small talk with casual acquaintances, I went for a morose walk and ended up at the John W. Weeks Footbridge that spanned the Charles River. I gazed at the glow of the "River Houses" (the upperclassman dorms closest to Harvard Yard), the sprawling opulence of Harvard Business School, and the shining lights of the city skyline off in the distance. I pondered the question I so often did: What if I were just one of those people destined always to be an outsider looking on?

I wasn't ready to concede defeat to loneliness, though, and I made a concerted effort to get involved in campus life in search of my people. Guest speakers, conferences, and events like the biannual "boot camp" for new members of Congress drew me often to the renowned John F. Kennedy School of Government, and an interest in volunteering led me to an open house hosted by the Phillips Brooks House Association. With a mission grounded in social justice and community engagement, PBHA was the largest public service organization at Harvard, an umbrella for dozens of programs—more than eighty to date—serving some 10,000 youth and adults.

At the open house, I volunteered to teach civics once a week for a semester in a Boston public school classroom. I am not sure what prompted me to sign up. Maybe it was memories of the conversations about current events in Mr. Osterweil's classroom or the political debates in Miss D's classroom, or the hope that the other Harvard students willing to volunteer to teach civics might just be my people. My instinct proved right.

Our weekly volunteer classes in Boston emphasized teaching students to collaborate in developing solutions to community challenges. PBHA Civics program leader David Wang also recruited me and a classmate named Eric Dawson to help bring a new program to kids called Peace Games, which would focus on conflict resolution. Peace Games was originally developed by University of Connecticut children's literature scholar Francelia Butler and focused on giving kids the opportunity to play cooperative—not just competitive—games.

Butler wanted to make sure the program lived on after her retirement and chose PBHA as a home and David Wang as the initial steward of her legacy.

For Eric, it would evolve into a twenty-five-year career devoted to combating school violence and promoting youth leadership. Eric was a laid-back scholarship kid from Columbus, Ohio, the son of parents who worked with high-risk youth and had instilled a deep sense of service in their son. He and I both soon became fixtures at Phillips Brooks House. I had found not only my tribe but my best friend.

We helped David recruit Boston and Cambridge schools to participate, flesh out the curriculum, train volunteer teachers, and organize the first PBHA-sponsored Peace Games festival, which brought hundreds of students to campus for a day of cooperative games.

Eric and I also spent a lot of our freshman spring raising $40,000 in donations to support our other passion project, which was to run one of PBHA's free summer tutoring and enrichment camps for kids living in Boston's most-impoverished neighborhoods.

And now we lived there, too, as part of PBHA's commitment to community involvement at the grassroots level. The Mission Main public housing project in the Mission Hill section of Roxbury (the historically African-American section of the city) was notorious in the 1990s as home to New England's largest open-air drug market at the height of the crack epidemic. The tightly packed blocks of dilapidated apartments sweltered without air-conditioning in the brutal heat and humidity of a Boston summer. Kids were more accustomed to the sounds of gunfire or sirens than the jingle of an ice cream truck. Our neighborhood had a little bodega a few blocks away, but no other amenities.

Unlike some of Boston's other public housing projects, the Mission Main Housing Development wasn't tucked away in an isolated corner of the city. Northeastern, Wentworth Institute of Technology, and the Harvard School of Public Health were all within walking distance, but their staff and students didn't venture into Mission Main and the people who lived in Mission Main didn't venture into those rarified spaces.

The walls of socioeconomic and racial segregation translated into the absence of a supermarket within walking distance or the essential businesses like barbershops, hair salons, banks and their ATMs, bakeries, newsstands, and coffee shops, which make day-to-day urban life healthier, easier, and more convivial.

If Mission Main buildings had a laundromat on the premises for tenants, the washers and dryers were more likely to be broken than working. Inside the subsidized homes, kitchen appliances were cheap and unreliable. Paint peeled, roaches and vermin proliferated unchecked, and complaints to anyone in power or with authority rarely resulted in any action. Mission Hill was maybe a thirty-minute drive from Cambridge in my used Toyota, but by every measure other than miles, the rows of squat brick buildings were a solar system or two away from the privilege, opportunity, and promise of Harvard Yard.

I'd never been happier in my life.

Eric and I shared our cramped, airless two-bedroom apartment with two other male classmates serving as senior counselors. There was a separate apartment in the next building over for the five female senior counselors. Our place was sparsely furnished with cast-off treasures foraged from campus dumpsters after the school year ended and everyone was in a hurry to clear out of the dorms. What didn't wobble was ripped, and what wasn't disgorging wads of stuffing was likely one strip of duct tape away from total collapse. We didn't have the space to be picky anyway, since we were operating a store that took over our living room (an oxymoron if ever there was one).

As co-director and the "money guy" of our summer camp, I was in charge of inventory, which consisted of the everyday school supplies that kids in our struggling neighborhood considered unattainable luxuries: composition books with marbled covers; jelly pencil boxes; Power Ranger and unicorn folders; tiny erasers shaped like pandas, skateboards, dinosaurs, hamburgers, and anything else tiny eraser makers could imagine—and, of course, glitter pens. We threw in some fun surprises as well—decks of UNO cards, coloring books, and markers that smelled like overripe strawberries. Prices were all in "ducats," which was the imperious name we gave the counterfeit currency we printed on a bubble jet and awarded to campers for good deeds, regular attendance, and completing their assignments.

Eric and I oversaw a team of seven senior counselors—all fellow college students, six from Harvard and one from Princeton—and eight junior counselors, who were mostly former campers ranging from fourteen to eighteen and hired through the Boston Parks and Recreation summer youth employment program. The number of campers that first summer hit sixty-four, ages six through thirteen, divided into eight groups (each with a senior counselor, including Eric, and a junior counselor). I was responsible for all the administrative activities like planning the big final field trips to Philadelphia and then DC, plus managing operations like getting breakfast and lunch distributed each day, or setting up the camp store. I was sort of dean of students, too, calming meltdowns over peer conflicts or from a traumatic event at home the night before.

I was also serving as vehicles coordinator for all the PBHA programs, an elected position that gave me both social and political currency as different groups jockeyed to schedule transportation to their fun field trips, important court dates, scholarship interviews, job fairs, immigration hearings, or whatever other service a PBHA program offered. One of our core missions was to provide ongoing assistance, to genuinely connect with the people and communities we served, rather than pop in and out for a onetime event. If providing kids a playground was a need, we wouldn't just raise money and hand over a check—PBHA would raise the money and engage parents and kids alike in discussions and decision making. The goal was to forge not just partnerships between the college and the community, but genuine relationships between the students and the residents. That was the toughest part.

Boston has long borne the reputation of being one of the most racist cities in America. When tensions combust, as they did, for example, when court-ordered school desegregation and busing triggered over forty riots between 1974 and 1976, the anger, hurt, and resentment lingered for years. Just a couple of years before I moved there, Mission Hill was the hot epicenter of national race division.

On the night of October 23, 1989, a man named Charles Stuart dialed 911 to report that he and his wife, Carol, had just been carjacked in Mission Hill by a Black man who shot them before fleeing. Police found the wounded white couple in their car. Charles, the twenty-nine-year-old manager of a fur store, had been shot in the stomach. His pregnant wife was slumped against him with a gunshot wound to the head. She didn't survive, and neither did the son who was delivered by emergency C-section at the hospital. Police launched a massive manhunt for the killer based on the dramatic account Charles provided, which was that a young African-American male in a black tracksuit had accosted the couple as they left a birthing class at Brigham and Women's Hospital. The man forced Charles at gunpoint to drive to Mission Hill, where he robbed and then shot the Stuarts before fleeing.

Boston police swarmed Mission Hill like storm troopers, kicking down doors, rounding up young Black males for interrogation, and conducting public "stop and frisk" searches without cause. Some men and teens were even told to drop their pants in public for a search. The county DA publicly called for reinstatement of the death penalty.

In late December, a man arrested and charged with robbing a video store was put in a police lineup and identified by Charles Stuart as the attacker. Within days, though, Stuart's siblings went to the police and implicated Charles himself, asserting that the carjacking was a hoax he had orchestrated after an earlier plan to stage a burglary for the insurance money failed. Before police could move in, Stuart left town and jumped from a bridge early the next morning, falling 135 feet to his death in the Mystic River. The falsely accused man's family received a visit and a personal apology from the mayor the next day. The trauma inflicted on the citizens of Mission Hill wasn't addressed.

Eric and I were too young and naive to appreciate what a leap of faith it took for the Mission Hill families to entrust their children to us—we were still just teenagers ourselves, and on the weighted side of the socioeconomic seesaw. Harvard was hope on a platter in a place where not even simple possibility was ever a given.

The longtime director of Phillips Brooks House, Greg Johnson, regularly and publicly criticized the university administration for not doing nearly enough for the communities in the shadow of its enormous prosperity, and just as regularly and publicly, the administration sought to oust him, framing the power struggle as a matter of liability. The risk of college students filling buses and vans with so-called "at-risk" children to take them on cultural and educational outings hours away from their even-riskier neighborhood was a financial burden and safety hazard Harvard was loath to bear. Especially since Harvard had no control over PBHA. The deans and accountants thought PBHA should focus on one-and-done charitable undertakings—like the meaningless two-hour "community service" field trip I remembered from Cherry Hill West High School, when we went to distribute gifts to kids at a rec center in a deeply impoverished section of Camden, New Jersey. I had been so enraged that I wrote about poverty tourism versus actual impact in my college admissions essay. Now the powers that be at Harvard wanted glossy photos of students doing public service that they could put in the brochure, but not the liability risk that came with deeper engagement. Greg thought they also didn't want the risk of students being transformed into activists by seeing inequities and injustices firsthand and then turning their organizing energy against Harvard.

Greg Johnson had come to Harvard as a freshman in 1968 and graduated with a degree in American history and literature in 1972. His first year alone had seen the escalation of the Vietnam War, police battling students in campus uprisings across the country, and the assassinations of civil rights leader and Nobel laureate Reverend Martin Luther King Jr. and presidential candidate Robert Kennedy. Greg's last three years included Woodstock, the Kent State massacre of student protesters by the National Guard, and the Watergate break-in. Greg came by his convictions about social justice by bearing witness, and he held the courage of his convictions with both fire and grace. He was deeply passionate about student leadership and service learning. Ten years at the helm of Phillips Brooks House had proven to him that serving others, learning from each other and from those we helped, would teach us how to become better people.

Greg Johnson instilled a sense of moral responsibility in the students who looked up to him as a role model, exhorting us to meaningfully address the needs of whichever community we proposed to serve by leaning into its stories. He urged every young idealist who passed through PBHA to dive beneath the surface and build intense relationships with the people whose lives we hoped to better. *Stay deeply engaged* was the mantra I took away with me.

Serving the Mission Hill community under Greg's tutelage was every bit as enlightening and informative for me as the class time I spent in one of my favorite courses at Harvard. The Literature of Social Reflection was taught by Dr. Robert Coles, an esteemed child psychiatrist and Pulitzer Prize–winning author who used poetry and literature to analyze human nature and our struggles over race, class, nationality, and identity. It was the magical confluence of words, thought, and actions from the syllabus of Dr. Coles and the philosophy of Greg Johnson that excited me most about my time at Harvard. On the ground and in the classroom, Greg and Dr. Coles pushed students to question: What systems operate to produce suffering in American society? How can those with privilege best help people in need, and is there a difference between help and genuine empowerment? How am I called to serve? From the day I set foot in Mr. Osterweil's class, acing a test or finishing an important assignment had always left me with a sense of deep satisfaction as a student. But that summer, I came to understand that real learning should always leave you hungry not just for knowledge but for true meaning. That meaning could be found in the relationships we built with kids, parents, and communities, as well as in the bonds we formed with the people alongside whom we served.

Our camp days at Mission Main were divided evenly between work and play. We spent mornings in the classroom, working to build on what the kids had learned during the school year with extra instruction in math and reading, science experiments, and lessons in African-American and Latino history. Afternoons were reserved for fun, games, and outings, including trips to cool down at a public pool. Counselors would be making ice cream and doing crafts with third graders one day and publishing a magazine with the eleven- and twelve-year-olds the next. Despite the university's ongoing efforts to clip our wings, the fleet of PBHA vans continued to shuttle campers who'd never left the Mission Hill neighborhood to museums, farms, concerts, the aquarium, and more.

Eric and I had spent long hours strategizing during the months leading up to camp, figuring out where to go for our "big" overnight field trip, whether we'd have time to see both the Liberty Bell and the Franklin Institute, and coordinating enough rooms for the kids to spend the night in a budget hotel for the first time. (In Philly, that meant claiming we were a family reunion, praying no one at check-in would question how two college guys came to be the patriarchs of a fifty-child clan.)

Our connections deepened with both the kids and their families. Though we were interlopers, we were never challenged by the drug dealers and gangs who reigned supreme in Mission Hill. While crime statistics would suggest otherwise, I never felt unsafe or in danger there. To the contrary, it felt like the parents of the community were protecting us—that our intentions were acknowledged as good, our commitment to the children genuine—and by some unspoken code, we were off-limits.

Every day, the counselors regrouped back at the apartment after camp, and kids would wander over just to hang out with us on the scruffy grass and dirt patch out front, laughing, listening to music, talking, and goofing around well into the evening. Counselors from other PBHA summer camps in different projects scattered across the city would often drop by, as well, and I began dating one of them. The junior counselors still in high school worked hard to impress the senior ones just barely out, peppering them with questions as they tried to decode whatever the secret map was that would lead them out of the projects. How did the counselors get into college? One of our roommates, Carey Gabay, had grown up in a working-class family in the North Bronx and had earned a scholarship to Harvard. Carey had a quiet kind of magnetism, with a sincerity and patience that didn't falter no matter how often the boys in his group tested it. He was invested in boys treating each other positively and being a team instead of posturing and stirring up trouble. He would take aside kids in conflict and convince them they were brothers who needed to take care of each other. When Carey spoke, they listened.

The camp provided breakfast and lunch for the kids, and we offered snacks and occasional treats, but we also knew that for some of the children, what we provided was their only guaranteed food for the day. If we got pizza after work, we learned to order enough to share with the kids who were never called in for supper, the ones like the six-year-old camper who lived in the building across from us and came over every day, never leaving until dark. "Would you like a slice?" I would offer, remembering too well what it felt like when my father had stopped going to the store. Seeing a child fall quiet and hang back when our food arrived reminded me of how desperately I had wanted someone to step in and understand what I needed when I couldn't find the words or the courage to ask.

Once the last stragglers had left, Eric and I used to debate our place in their lives, talking deep into the night about where the personal boundaries of public service are when boundaries are the very thing you're striving to break down in society. Questions that Mr. Osterweil, Miss D, and their colleagues may have asked themselves about me. How do you connect without becoming emotionally entangled, when do you intervene, when do you just listen? What about Leah, the student whose only goal was to make it to her birthday without having a baby, because no female in her family had made it past fifteen before becoming a mother? Would we be able to persuade Leah that her fate wasn't sealed? That the subsidized apartment that motherhood might bring wasn't the only passport to freedom and adulthood? The female counselors spent long hours in deep conversation with Leah, telling her about all the choices waiting for her, exciting goals that could be hers, because she did deserve them and she could achieve them.

Living in the community and not just driving in, we came to know the families, and their problems, more deeply, and we became invested in both. The hyper ten-year-old's non-stop antics for attention weren't a nuisance when you knew it was an open secret in the neighborhood that his dad had more than one family. The working mother Eric befriended wasn't incapable or unwilling to properly care for her children; she wanted only the best for them. She was overwhelmed by her own live-in mother's mental health problems, which culminated in her setting their apartment on fire. Eric helped the family access social services and other programs to provide the interventions they needed.

While I studied the intricacies and challenges of governing and creating public policy in the classroom, among our campers and their families, I could clearly see how incredibly smart,

talented people can be crushed or lifted up and out of circum-
stances they couldn't control. Mission Hill children had witnessed people getting killed. They had watched people they
knew and ones they loved get locked up for years over a crack
pipe found in a stop-and-frisk. They saw grade school friends
they played pickup basketball with on courts with rusty, netless
hoops morph into street-smart peers by middle school, stealing
the bicycles or boom boxes they wanted to win the approval of
the gang members and drug lords who would put them on their
payroll soon enough.

What saddened me the most was how inevitable it seemed for
so many kids to repeat the same horrific cycle their older siblings, parents, and even grandparents had. It wasn't always a simple question of whether they would choose the right path given
the right intervention; sometimes the wrong path stole their lives
right out from under them, overwhelmed them, and took away
choice.

Selling drugs isn't necessarily the choice a sixteen-year-old
makes because he wants to make more money than he can at
McDonald's to buy an expensive Nintendo system or designer
sneakers. Watching life unfold in Mission Hill, I saw in real time
that selling drugs is also a choice a sixteen-year-old might make
because the single parent raising him plus three siblings is struggling with addiction and can't work. Public assistance doesn't
always stretch far enough to feed, clothe, and take care of an
entire household, so it falls on the oldest child to get the most
money the quickest way. And for the little sister just behind him,
getting pregnant in the eighth grade isn't a shame, it's a path.

By our third year at Harvard, I was serving as PBHA president
and Eric was on the board. The AP credits I had stockpiled in

high school were enough for me to graduate early, and my final semester delivered a reality lesson in policy and politics.

Harvard launched yet another reevaluation of the role of public service on campus as a thinly veiled maneuver to simultaneously undermine PBHA's student-led independence, make the programming less meaningful (and therefore less risky in the minds of the guardians of institutional interests), and push Greg out. I joined the battle to save Greg Johnson's job. It was my first taste of navigating a hostile bureaucracy in pursuit of a just cause. Making arguments to the deans and faculty members charged with protecting Harvard's interests over those of the community reconnected me with my high school activism. Whether buttonholing them on the fly between classes, speaking up at public meetings, or writing letters, I tried to help them see not only the positive impact we were having in the neighborhoods of Boston and Cambridge, but how vital the experiences were to the Harvard education of thousands of students and alumni. PBHA was the embodiment of Harvard's pursuit of truth and excellence, not a distraction from it, I argued. At the end of the year, I would have to pass the baton in the fight over Greg's role and the future governance of PBHA, but as I prepared to set forth on my own career path, his clarity and commitment inspired me.

Gil visited me on campus that senior year, and I was eager to show my brother the place where my life had finally begun. He was now in his thirties but still unsettled. He and Michelle had broken up for good, and Gil was living in Virginia. He was drunk the entire weekend, making a fool of himself and embarrassing me as he crudely hit on women I considered my peers, but he stereotyped as "pretty coeds" hurrying past us on the sidewalk. At dinner one night with my friends, Eric started baiting

Gil in a cool, laconic style that I knew concealed points as sharp as bayonets. I seethed with silent anger at them both. At Eric for humiliating Gil, at Gil for humiliating me. I still didn't want to let Gil go. I chose him still. He came to visit because he wanted to see his little brother at Harvard, and I knew he was proud.

My grandmother, Uncle Hal, and Aunt Jean came to my graduation. I could see the pride in my grandmother's smiles and happy tears. Her courageous decision to leave a bad marriage and Puerto Rico behind to seek opportunity in the Bronx had made that moment possible. I hoped that Uncle Hal and Aunt Jean knew that their kind intervention was beginning to pay off; not all the wayward family members they took in over the years got back on track, but they had helped me find my way. After just three years thanks to all those AP classes, I left Harvard with my bachelor of arts degree with a concentration in government, unaware of where it would eventually take me. But all the choices that lay before me had crystallized into one conviction: I knew now exactly where I fit into the greater mosaic, what I wanted to do for the rest of my life.

I would teach.

CHAPTER SIX

My first year of teaching remains, to this day, the most difficult job I ever held.

Every grand plan and great hope, each carefully considered objective and overanalyzed option, and every idealistic notion I harbored about having a classroom of my own—all evaporated like a drop of rain in the Sahara before I even finished out my first week as the new history teacher on the second floor.

I was lucky enough to leave Harvard with two coveted awards. The Truman Scholarship was for students who want to pursue careers in government, the nonprofit sector, or elsewhere in public service. It provided me with prize money I could apply toward graduate school and leadership development programs. The highly competitive James Madison Memorial Fellowship offered scholarships to current and prospective secondary social studies teachers passionate about teaching the US Constitution. The latter would cover my tuition at Columbia University's

Teachers College. I left Cambridge full speed ahead to settle in New York City and spend a year earning my master of arts in the teaching of social studies.

Everything felt like a beginning that summer. The future I yearned for was within sight. I moved with my college girlfriend, Debbie—who had been another student leader at Phillips Brooks House—into a Harlem apartment across from Central Park, for the first time owning actual furniture. I was still too young to toast the milestone. I was twenty years old, taking a full course load, student teaching, and trying, always, to plan what would come next, and next, and next. There seemed to be so much more urgency and importance to life all of a sudden. As a nation, we ushered in a new era: We witnessed the first Million Man March in Washington DC and the final concert by the Grateful Dead. Consumers welcomed AOL, eBay, and Sony PlayStations into their homes. The bombing of a federal building in Oklahoma City killed 168 people in the country's deadliest act of domestic terror to date.

For much of 1995, though, a single topic dominated the headlines: the divisive murder trial of Hall of Fame football star O. J. Simpson. The full courtroom proceedings in Los Angeles were being broadcast live—a first—and like a live-action soap opera, they held an entire nation in thrall. Overheard chatter on the subway or sidewalks, colleagues spending breaks gathered around the TV in the lunchroom, family gatherings, social events—the trial sparked a running national commentary full of searing questions about social justice and systemic racism. I spent that year living intensely inside my own head, pondering my role as an educator as most new teachers do. What part might I play someday in forging a truly equitable America? How would I find my place as a teacher in such a quest?

At Columbia, many of my classmates were already working teachers getting their graduate degrees, some even pursuing a second MA or PhD. To accommodate so many students trying to juggle jobs and school, many courses were scheduled in the evening or late afternoon. That suited me perfectly, because it cleared most of my day for student teaching. It was traditional to fulfill those required hours in the spring semester, but I wanted to squeeze more out of my assignment, to treat it like a year-long internship and gain as much hands-on experience as possible. After running the camp at Mission Hill and volunteering as an after-school tutor there throughout the year, I was eager to be with kids again. I was assigned to student-teach at Beacon High School.

Beacon was a small public high school with a central core built around technology and the arts. When enrollment opened, eager parents would line up by the hundreds to pick up application packets at the century-old converted warehouse blocks from Columbus Circle in Manhattan. Aspiring students underwent a rigorous review of their "portfolios," which included their best coursework from middle school, essays, recommendations, and interviews. Impressively, while New York City's "admission by exam" schools like Stuyvesant served vanishingly few Black and Latino students, Beacon's multiple-measures application process yielded a racially and socioeconomically diverse student population. Classes at Beacon were small, and the learning process was designed to be creative, interactive, and vigorous. The school was adjacent to the Lincoln Center campus of Fordham University's School of Education, the very institution where my parents first met as professor and student. Beacon was the kind of school where fencing and bowling were perfectly viable alternatives to basketball and soccer, a place where educational travel opportunities might take students to India during one break and Sweden the next. My goal was to someday teach broad survey courses like US history on the high school level, and Beacon paired me with a team of veteran faculty members teaching just that. Bayard Faithfull and Harry Streep III (brother of actress Meryl) welcomed me warmly when I began that October and quickly became valuable mentors to me.

Young and as inexperienced as I was, I still was made to feel very much a part of the faculty, encouraged to ask questions and share ideas. There was no cafeteria at Beacon, so we would all just bring our lunches or get carryout to eat back in the classroom along with whichever students were doing the same. Occasionally, I remembered to pack some leftovers, but more often than not a sandwich (turkey, Swiss, mustard) and chips from a neighborhood bodega had to suffice. Within the country's largest public school system, Beacon felt like a sheltered cove.

Harry, a trained dancer who also coached basketball, had a gift for offering feedback that was gentle but always cut to the chase. On the day I was scheduled to fly solo for the first time, I was supposed to present a lesson on the Spanish-American War and early colonialism in the Caribbean. The assignment excited me, and I spent a ton of time meticulously planning out my lesson and preparing for the class. I scoped out a very clear objective, gathered different visuals (photographs, maps, political cartoons), and compiled the primary source documents I wanted to use, like a newspaper editorial from the era. I came into class that day brimming with confidence.

I tanked.

It was a terrible, tedious hour that felt like ten, and I could see the mind-numbing boredom on my students' faces. Harry, observing, channeled Oscar-winning acting genes just to look neutral instead of stupefied. What I delivered was a lecture with materials: Here is an exciting visual to look at from afar, here is some exciting material to read quietly to yourselves in class, here is me telling an exciting story, and me again still talking. I was disheartened to see how thoroughly disengaged everyone was at the end: heads down on desks, eyes directed to the windows rather than the board or even peers, and none of the energy or buzz that comes with rich discussion.

"You know," Harry ventured after class was dismissed, "you figured out the lesson by thinking of all the things you were going to do, but you need to always plan with what your *students* are going to do. If you did that, you would have seen that they weren't doing anything for an hour except listening to you present."

He was right. And embarrassed as I was, I was eager to show him I got it.

When we came to a lesson on the Cuban revolution, I jumped at the chance to teach it like an overzealous insurgent promised a bullhorn and a crowd. I went out and bought an army fatigue jacket at a secondhand store, along with a brimmed cloth field cap from the Che Guevara line. I completed my scavenger hunt with a fake beard and a fat cigar. The next day, Fidel Castro strode into the classroom, Spanish accent (my grandmother's) and all. I announced a press conference, told the students they were the reporters, and invited them to ask me whatever questions they wanted—informed, of course, by the reading they had done. They loved it.

So did I. I had always enjoyed theater and class plays during my own school days, and Fidel was a much juicier role than being a flower in *Alice in Wonderland*. I hammed it up to the hilt, ranting about the American trade embargo between puffs of my cigar, boasting about Cuba's high literacy level, indignantly shutting down any question about dissent. *"We don't talk about that!"*

Every student was engaged, laughing at my antics and challenging me to debate various issues. It was a rollicking lesson, and the hour flew by.

I was excited to see how easily I could bring history alive and infect indifferent teenagers with my enthusiasm for the subject, and Harry's smile made it even more gratifying. Not long after, he asked me to cover his modern dance class when he had to be out. I approached it with the same bravado and brought my sweats to school. Fortunately, I also brought some common sense and acceptance of my own limitations; I was young and reasonably fit, but I was no Alvin Ailey. I wisely selected a couple of star pupils to lead us through the steps, and I participated as best I could, all of us cracking up at my struggle to keep up.

The real lesson for me at Beacon was the same whether I was on a dance floor or steering a class discussion, and I realized it was exactly what made my years with Mr. Osterweil and Miss D so transformative. Teaching was more than just conveying information to your students; it was about connecting with them and clearing the path with just the right mix of foundational skills and knowledge. Meaningful hands-on learning opportunities and scaffolded support help them build knowledge on their own. It's about showing and sharing your joy—the musicality of learning.

The knowledge I gleaned at Teachers College came from my fellow students as well as the professors there. My concentration in teaching social studies put me in classes with people who shared my eagerness to reflect on race, racial identity, and social change. There were interesting tensions in those honest discussions. Columbia is an urban university, yet all of the tenured faculty members in our department were white, and many of my classmates were headed to jobs in the suburbs. I was very focused on educating low-income students of color, and with my undergrad degree in government and fascination with creating and implementing policy, I really wanted to harness education as a vehicle for advancing social justice.

Some of my classmates shared a similar dream. Soon, I was ensconced in a tight little community of aspiring educators supporting, encouraging, and challenging each other. Going to the movies or grabbing brunch with new friends could turn into a bracing daylong discussion of what the ideal school and curriculum might be. It was this mood of exploration and discovery that made a surprising idea take root in my imagination.

What if I spent my first year of teaching in Puerto Rico? I could explore the island, learn more about my cultural identity, immerse myself in the local community, and improve my Spanish. It was the familiar orphan voice within, that nagging lifelong hunger to find myself, that urged me to pack up my belongings and go.

My girlfriend, Debbie, was chasing her own dream of medical school and had no interest in temporarily relocating to Puerto Rico. We parted sadly but amicably, and I arrived in San Juan not knowing a soul.

The island culture of my imagination was infused with the vibrancy of my mother and my grandmother, further enhanced by my brother Gil's memories of happy summers spent working at his father's popular restaurant. Given my experiences in the Mission Hill projects and at Beacon High School, I blithely assumed that faculty, students, and parents at St. John's would fold me just as quickly and easily into the school's culture. They, in turn, assumed I knew what I was doing.

We were both wrong.

As a first-year teacher, there's no warm-up lap. We don't arrive with a year's stockpile of lesson plans or course material we've already road-tested. There aren't fat files of vocabulary lists, pre-drafted projects, scripted simulations, or sure-fire questions to ignite discussion. For all our theorizing about curriculum, at Teachers College we never created an actual quiz or test. We never formally studied how best to design test questions, or even talked about how to accurately assess what our students had learned. We were never locked in a room for rainy-day recess with thirty rambunctious youngsters. Only accrued experience and wisdom will hone the skills to keep a rowdy classroom from devolving into adolescent anarchy. There's no college credit for a psychology course on difficult parents, either. How does a twenty-one-year-old rookie teacher command respect from a forty-two-year-old helicopter mom? I wish I had an answer. Or at least a punch line.

The same great unknown that seemed so exciting in theory in a classroom at Columbia was, in fact, utterly terrifying in person in a classroom in San Juan. Student teaching, it turned out, is a lot like riding a bike with training wheels—it doesn't really count. And this time, I didn't have any mentors like Harry Streep to pick me up when I crashed.

My intention to get in touch with my roots appeared like-wise doomed. Even though I am 50 percent Puerto Rican, in San Juan, I was regarded merely as 100 percent outsider. I was the darkest person in a predominantly "white" school for Puerto Rico's elite and wealthy mainlanders and international students. To be fair, my colleagues weren't overtly hostile. To do that, they would have had to actually regard me. Besides being dark-skinned and from the mainland, I was the only first-year teacher in the secondary school, and the only other faculty member from the mainland had been there for a while. It was clear that the cliquish older faculty already had their established relationships. There wasn't any coffee-and-doughnuts type of structure to make me feel welcomed, either. I was deflated to discover that the principal's idea of orientation was pretty much, *Here are your textbooks.* In the faculty lounge, I could politely sidle my way into casual conversations, but no one invited me home for dinner or offered sightseeing suggestions, let alone an actual outing. I wasn't expecting *Fodor's,* but I hadn't anticipated *Lonely Planet,* either. On the bright side, I had lucked out on the real estate front and scored an affordable oceanfront apartment to rent. I would need that Zen.

At a school like St. John's, everybody basically does their work, and the kids were genuinely welcoming. They were happy to have a young teacher. My degrees from Harvard and Columbia impressed them, and I loved being able to offer juniors and seniors practical advice that was actually current when they peppered me with questions about getting into their top-choice schools. Most of them planned to leave the island for college. In my US history classroom, some of my eleventh graders lit up when I used the hard parts of American history—slavery, taking land from Indigenous people, Japanese internment camps during World War II, Jim Crow—to ask about systemic oppression in the present tense, what was happening in their own time, on their own island. When we examined the evolution of African-American cultural traditions in the context of slavery, students talked about their experiences visiting Loíza, a Puerto Rican town whose history was shaped by the West African enslaved people the Spanish brought to the island, and their cultural fusion with the indigenous Tainos.

By comparison, my exchanges with colleagues in the faculty lounge were like trying to chug sour milk to slake a deep thirst. Any attempt I made to broach discussion about race and diversity in Puerto Rico was waved off with dismissive insistence that Puerto Ricans didn't think of race the same way the mainland did. After a while, I stopped trying and resigned myself to polite small talk.

Being only a few years older than the high school seniors gave me generational relevance but also made me vulnerable. I went into the job worrying that my youth would be a liability, but in fact, it was the glue in the bond the kids formed with me.

One afternoon in particular solidified it.

Puerto Rico was a buggy place. Insects I had never seen before made cameo appearances in my personal space every day. I quickly realized that I was vastly outnumbered and would poison myself before I successfully eradicated them with bug spray. I was learning to adjust my boundaries and coexist with them somewhat peacefully. One afternoon, while reading a few lines to the class from a book held in front of my face, I glanced up and was gratified to see that the students were paying rapt attention. What I didn't realize was that all that attention was actually going to a large beetle-like bug slowly making its way up the spine of the book I was holding. When it climbed over the top and onto the page I was reading, I shrieked and flung the book into the air. The kids, of course, erupted in gales of hysterical laughter. They never let me live down the Miss Muffet moment, but at the end of the day, I was grateful for the inside joke and the bond it created between us. I could always count on classrooms full of teenagers to carry on the work Denauvo had begun to make me lighten up.

Connecting with the parents, however, seemed as lost a cause as connecting with my colleagues.

We were maybe six weeks into the semester when the principal buttonholed me one afternoon and said matter-of-factly, "Hey, John, tomorrow night we have parent-teacher conferences. Good luck!" I had no idea what I was supposed to do. We had never talked about parent engagement at Teachers College, and I had never experienced parent-teacher conferences as a student teacher. My only real exposure to parent-teacher conferences was an episode of the TV sitcom *Growing Pains*, where Mike Seaver, the slacker teenage son, gets into some kind of trouble and his parents are called in for a parent-teacher conference. I remembered that the teacher had pushed a few desks into a circle, and that his desk had a stack of papers (presumably Mike's "permanent file") on it. I staged a similar setup in my classroom, grabbing a bunch of random papers that had nothing to do with anything and stacking them on my desktop. That was as ready as I knew how to get.

The first parents came in, and we all sat awkwardly looking at each other. Other than introducing myself, I was at a loss as to how this all worked. The only theme that emerged from the stream of equally strained meetings was that the parents thought I was grading my quizzes too hard. I was proud that I had managed to create any quizzes at all. Just preparing lessons was an exhausting, nonstop hamster wheel marathon for me. I came to the job thinking I would use a bit of weekend time to prepare a week's worth of lesson plans in one shot, but the reality was that I was up all night, every night, doing it. I never got enough sleep. It was like perpetually cramming for a final exam, only to discover there was another final the next day, and every weekday after that. Just having materials in hand to teach my students was a major accomplishment and worth a spot on the Olympic podium.

In addition to my regular course load at St. John's, I had volunteered to teach an after-school enrichment course on one of my favorite topics, the US Constitution. The Constitution fascinated me at its most basic level as our forefathers' ultimate achievement in policymaking, creating a foundation that not only endures after more than two hundred years, but continues to inspire as society confronts the challenges of an ever-changing world. Just before coming to Puerto Rico, I had attended the James Madison Memorial Fellowship Foundation Summer Institute at American University in Washington DC. For a month, I immersed myself in the Mayflower Compact and other early governing documents of the American colonies. I traced the road to the Declaration of Independence and the American Revolution and weighed the inadequacy of the Articles of Confederation. I pored over the debates at the Constitutional Convention, the arguments between the Federalists and Anti-Federalists, and the early implementation of the US Constitution. I reveled in the company of my peers: fifty or so nerdy history teachers—one from each state and territory, some liberal, some conservative, but all passionate about government, philosophy, and economics. As far as I was concerned, it was the summer of 1787. I became more awestruck than ever by the thought and effort that went into creating a national government that shared power with the states and safeguarded the individual liberties of every American. There was an unparalleled elegance and economy to those 4,543 immortal words (7,591 with the 27 amendments).

Our fellowship included several field trips to historic sites significant to the study of the Constitution. One of those was Monticello, the 5,000-acre plantation and primary home of Thomas Jefferson in the rolling green hills of Charlottesville, Virginia. I was very conscious that the focus of that trip was supposed to be on Jefferson the statesman and author of the Declaration of Independence, and I valued the opportunity to reflect with my Madison cohort on the role Jefferson played in shaping the nation. But as the day wore on, I couldn't shake the feeling that the ground we were walking on was not just sacred or hallowed, but simultaneously horrific, soaked in the blood and tears of over four hundred individuals Jefferson enslaved at Monticello over generations, among them Sally Hemings, the young teenaged girl he raped and forced to bear six children, none given their father's name.

The field trip was my first time knowingly visiting a plantation, and I found it more jarring than I had anticipated. Amid the celebration of undeniable American exceptionalism and Jefferson's unquestionable brilliance, I felt a profound sense of sadness thinking about what the people enslaved there had endured, what it meant to be viewed by the law as having no rights, less than fully human. I imagined lives of endless toil under the threat of the lash or worse, the pain of children ripped away from their parents to be sold off, likely never to see them again.

On the bus back to American University, I tried to keep my tone scholarly and neutral as I sought to stir discussion about the tensions between Jefferson's writings on freedom and the legalities of holding fellow human beings in bondage, as he had done. Throughout that summer, I had been mindful to come across as raising provocative questions about race, but not to make myself the center of attention; it was important to me to be seen as intellectually curious but friendly, affable, and a good listener. I didn't want to be seen as angry, though that day at Monticello, I was deeply so. Although I loved studying the founders and the evolution of American democracy, I wished for a fuller, more honest conversation about where America had fallen short of its promise—not just in that summer's classes but ultimately in the teaching of American history across the country. I was committed to making my classroom one where we would grapple, together as teacher and students, with hard truths.

I had expected maybe four or five serious students at St. John's to sign up for my once-a-week enrichment course, which I intended to be a forum for honestly discussing the complexity of American constitutional history through famous legal cases that helped shape it. But ten to fifteen students would routinely show up and enthusiastically participate. The rhythm of first-year teaching is that you can have a day where you feel like you just hit a tie-breaking, game-winning home run in the bottom of the ninth inning, and on that very same day, you also feel like Bill Buckner of the Red Sox letting Mookie Wilson's slow ground ball slip between your legs, breathing new life into the 1986 Mets on their road to winning the World Series.

My biggest goal was to get my students excited and interested in history, to feed their sense of curiosity, to get them hooked on connecting the dots between the past and the present. I hadn't fully anticipated the degree to which the Supreme Court would lend me a hand, but that fire I was looking for was lit one drowsy afternoon when I introduced a landmark case—later largely overturned—about freedom of speech and the Espionage Act of 1917.

US Supreme Court Justice Oliver Wendell Holmes wrote the majority opinion upholding the conviction of Charles Schenck, a socialist whose distribution of handbills opposing military conscription was deemed "a clear and present danger" to the government. (Holmes's opinion famously alluded to falsely shouting "fire" in a crowded theater.) Everyone in the class immediately started talking over each other. A girl named Maria-Cristina, usually among the most reserved, was suddenly among the most vehement. Of course, for teenagers finding their voice with adults at school and adults at home, few topics are as compelling as the right to "say what you want, when you want, and where you want" and constraints on that right.

It was a highlight of my year at St. John's, but in truth, although those moments of student outrage and awakening that I craved were frequent, I feared they weren't enduring. The reality was that the institution itself was part of a deeply entrenched social hierarchy—the mission of St. John's was far more preservation of the status quo than playing a role as a transformative force for the social good. From my students' comments in class and my colleagues' comments in the faculty lounge, I could tell how rare it was for students to reflect in their other classes on the island's intense income inequality, the role of the color line in disparate access to opportunity, or the complicated relationship between the mainland United States and Puerto Rico. Discussion of civic and social responsibility was similarly rare, and there was no

PBHA-like effort to deeply engage students in public service in Puerto Rican communities in need. My students would inherit not just their families' wealth but their dominance of Puerto Rican business and politics, and I worried that the school wasn't inculcating a sense of moral responsibility for using that power to tackle inequality and injustice on the island.

When I went home for Christmas break, I felt defeated and disillusioned. I had underestimated how all-consuming first-year teaching would be and how little time I would have to immerse myself in Puerto Rican life and culture. And I had misread what teaching at St. John's would be like. There was neither the social justice spirit nor the camaraderie of the Mission Hill Summer Program, Teachers College, or Beacon High School. The King family was gathered for the holidays in Florida, where Uncle Hal and Aunt Jean were wintering. The usual pandemonium and joy wrapped around me like a warm blanket, providing such a counterpoint to the loneliness and exclusion I felt in San Juan that I began entertaining the idea of not going back. Chatting in the kitchen one night with family members, someone asked what I had planned for New Year's back in San Juan. "*If* I go back," I offhandedly replied.

My cousin Hal, an Air Force veteran some thirty years my senior with a Harvard MBA, immediately homed in on me.

"What do you mean *if*?" There were still six months left on my one-year contract.

Hal had always felt more like my older, wiser brother than a cousin. Like his father, my Uncle Hal, he knew how to listen between the lines and cut to the chase.

"I'm really unhappy and thinking of not going back," I confided. I poured it all out—how much I had wanted to become part of a community in Puerto Rico, how I missed that kind of connection I had found with Eric and Carey in Mission Hill or Bayard and Harry at Beacon, and how I resented that St. John's didn't have it. I genuinely liked the kids, but I still felt socially isolated and frustrated. I wanted to *know* Puerto Rico, but my job didn't afford me much free time to explore and embed myself in the community.

The downside of my beachfront apartment in the touristy area around the school instead of one in a more mixed part of town was that it deprived me of a neighborhood and local hangouts where I might have had better luck finding Puerto Ricans my age and practicing my Spanish. I would go to the movies once in a while with my neighbor, a white Midwesterner in the military who was gone a lot. My main social outlet was vicarious: The laundromat in my building was right next to a little food counter and bar, and the walls were thin enough to hear voices on the other side. Eavesdropping while my towels dried and piecing together Spanish banter about sports, the government, or how bad the roads were felt a little like sitting in the barbershop in Cambridge while I was at Andover, a comforting access to point to a piece of my identity. But that was just a window on life in Puerto Rico, not a set of genuine relationships. I depended on friends visiting from the mainland to feel a sense of connection.

"I hear you, and I get all of that," my cousin told me, "and sometimes you're going to have experiences in your professional and personal life that are really hard. But how would you feel about yourself if you quit versus how you would feel if you stuck it out and went back with a sense of resolve?"

"The students will be fine," I replied, feeling defensive, "and the school will be fine."

"That's not the point," he shot back. "The point is how are you going to define yourself? Are you going to be the person who gives up, or the person who figures out how to keep the commitment?"

There was no need to remind me that this was the King family tradition we were really talking about—pressing through adversity. Intelligence, focus, and hard work all mattered, but success was determined by your character.

I returned to San Juan and kept my promise.

——————

After my one-year commitment was completed at St. John's, I spent the summer interning at the US Department of Education (ED) in Washington. The high-level internship was a core element of the Truman scholarship I was awarded while I was at Harvard. Going to the office every day, I felt recharged watching policy take shape at the highest level of government and witnessing the dedication of role models like Terry Dozier.

Terry was formerly named National Teacher of the Year. She was a wildly popular world history teacher from South Carolina who had been made a special adviser to the secretary of education, Richard Riley. She was the stand-in for educators across America when the politicians around the table needed a reminder that policy was meant to serve the people, not the other way around. Hers was a new and unique role at ED, and I admired the way she calibrated passion and purpose so effortlessly, never letting ego throw her off course.

Male politicos overwhelmingly populated the tables she sat at, but Terry recognized that being an outsider was what made her perspective so valuable. She leaned into the role with confidence and conviction. She focused keenly on how each minute detail of some new mandate might impact the teachers and administrators carrying it out, and how it would benefit the children at the end of the day. I quietly noted the kind of finesse it took to be the voice for others when decisions were being made and lives impacted. Terry carried it off without kowtowing to anyone or decimating egos in the process.

As my internship drew to a close, I realized that, for once, there was no preloaded next step to my life. I could go anywhere, be anyone. Put my finger on the map and find a school that was looking for a social studies teacher. Maybe I was just risk-averse after my dreams got dashed in Puerto Rico, or maybe my inner compass naturally pointed to urban environments instead of the Alaskan bush or the Everglades, but the place that ended up calling to me most was the very one I had left in search of my "real life."

Boston.

The fall before I left, the city had been the launching pad for a bold state initiative to reform public schools, where inequitable funding and lax standards were systematically denying an adequate education to children in low-income, largely Black and Latino communities. Besides ensuring that all school districts would have sufficient funding regardless of their community's wealth or tax base, the sweeping legislation set a higher bar for student achievement and held each school and district accountable for meeting it. The biggest news was that it created charter schools, making the Commonwealth of Massachusetts among the first in the country to do so. Charter schools were publicly funded but led by an independent board of trustees accountable to the state rather than a school district. In return for greater autonomy in curriculum and operations, the schools are given a five-year contract to deliver on the promises in their charter applications.

After a rigorous application process, the state's first fourteen charters had opened their doors in the fall of 1995. Among them was one just blocks from Mission Hill. City on a Hill was the only charter founded and managed by teachers, a distinction that immediately piqued my interest. The founders, Sarah Kass and Ann Connolly Tolkoff, set forth a challenging program that would grant diplomas only to students who were judged competent in each discipline by juries from diverse professional backgrounds. Students were admitted to the charters by lottery, and in its first year, 147 applicants vied for 65 spots at City on a Hill. Competition was even tougher for teachers: Over 350 applied for just three open slots that first year. Pay was in line with that of a district schoolteacher—low—but the pressure to perform was conversely high, since renewing the charter was directly linked to proving academic success.

Sarah and Ann didn't make it easy on themselves, either: Besides proficiency in the fundamentals of reading, writing, math, and science, City on a Hill students would not graduate unless, among other things, they could converse in a second language, deliver a 10-to-15-minute public speech, analyze primary documents in history, defend their views on contemporary issues, use technology for learning, and swim. The latter challenge was taken up by the city's central YMCA, which also housed the new school, providing ten classrooms.

I settled back into my familiar circles in Boston, sharing an apartment in Somerville with Eric, reconnecting with old Harvard friends still in the area. I applied for teaching jobs at a number of schools, but had my hopes set on City on a Hill. I was excited that the charter included a civic mission to create engaged citizenship, getting students invested in both their own futures and their communities. They would be required to engage in public service and would be assigned internships with professional partners in courtrooms, hospitals, museums, newspapers, nonprofits, and government agencies. It sounded like the perfect antidote to the lingering sense of disappointment about St. John's lack of a culture of civic engagement that I had carried back from Puerto Rico. I was thrilled when I was offered a job teaching history in a department that would total two members as soon as I came aboard.

By my second year, I was promoted to head of the history department. I recruited and hired two more faculty members. One of them, Teresa Rodriguez, was a true kindred spirit, and the friendship we instantly struck up was destined to last a lifetime. Teresa was the type of teacher whose fervor was contagious. She was tenacious about getting students and parents to come see her before school, during lunch, after school—whatever it took to make sure kids had both the academic and emotional support they needed. Her open door and open heart drew everyone in, and I was never surprised to pop by her classroom and find kids hanging out just to talk long after a tutoring session had ended. We were both working crazy hours. Once the school day and after-hours tutoring officially ended, Teresa and I would stay to prep for the next day and grade papers, taking a snack break at dinnertime to grab a bag of Sour Patch Kids. I usually left close to nine at night, returning at seven the following morning. I kept a box of Crispy Wheats 'n Raisins cereal in my car with a plastic bowl so I could eat breakfast on the drive to school.

The jury system of assessing progress and achievement meant that City on a Hill students could be in different grades for different classes if they didn't meet the standards. Teachers tried to provide lots of support, including tutoring and homework help available every day after school—and sometimes even on Saturdays.

Ricardo was a student who needed that extra support. He was the kid who never seemed to be paying attention, never did any of the homework assignments, and was perpetually hanging on to the lowest D-minus possible. But if I called on him, he'd have some brilliant insight. He inevitably turned in a mountain of makeup work at the very last minute. He was usually in a different grade in every subject, depending how far he'd fallen behind. He was in my eleventh grade history class—having passed my tenth grade class with a 59.5 rounded to a 60. When I assigned the class a paper on any figure who inspired them from the Great Migration and Harlem Renaissance era, I was surprised when Ricardo chose Marcus Garvey. The controversial Jamaican-born political activist is a complex research project, which didn't bode well for Ricardo's style. But Ricardo was infatuated with the concept of Black excellence and Black community self-determination, and I was heartened to see him so excited. It took him a few tries to put together an outline, and I was pleased when he asked for some after-school help with his first draft. As it happened, I was pondering self-determination myself at the moment, debating whether it was time to leave the classroom after the semester ended.

The sister of my old college girlfriend, Debbie, had reached out to me to have dinner and meet her then-boyfriend (now husband), Evan Rudall, who had recently graduated from

Harvard's Graduate School of Education and hoped to start his own charter school. He wanted to pick my brain. We met at an Indian restaurant and spent the next three or four hours talking about education, bouncing ideas, philosophies, and dreams off each other. We shared an ideal of top-tier public education providing the momentum for a cultural, intellectual, and economic Black renaissance in Roxbury and similar communities deprived of the opportunities a college degree brings. Fewer than 10 percent of adults held bachelor's degrees in Roxbury at the time.

Evan was going to submit his charter application the following day. He later told me he pulled an all-nighter to rework his proposal and incorporate my ideas about the planning time, professional development, and collaboration around teaching and learning I wished had been more deeply embedded at City on a Hill.

When Evan later got his charter for Roxbury Prep, he called me with the good news. We stayed in touch and became friends, and our running conversation about the new school ultimately led him to invite me to be co-founding co-director. The first class of sixth graders would be arriving in the fall. Designing a curriculum and running a school from the ground up was a captivating idea, but the tempting offer came at a great cost. I wasn't sure I could give up the classroom so soon. I would be changing lanes, becoming a middle school administrator instead of a high school social studies teacher. Also, did I really want to pour my heart and soul into a venture that could easily fail?

The first batch of charters in Massachusetts, including City on a Hill, were years shy of their prove-it-or-lose-it five-year trial period. It was 1999 and the waters were still untested.

While I agonized over Evan's proposition, Ricardo had turned our after-school tutoring sessions into a standing meeting. I had never seen him work so diligently. He soldiered through multiple drafts of his report, his enthusiasm growing with each revision, his resolve strengthening every time I pointed out the weak spots and pushed him to dig deeper into his demanding subject. Ricardo was doing his final polish with me one afternoon when he suddenly looked up from his paper.

"You know, Mr. King, I just wish I'd known in ninth grade what I know now," he lamented. "I get it now, what it takes to be a good student and be academically successful, and I'm really enjoying it. I just wish now I was in position to graduate on time and go to college, but I made so many mistakes."

Just like that, a sixteen-year-old who teetered on the edge of failure, barely scraping by, made one of the most important decisions of my life for me. This was the answer I'd been searching for while stalling Evan: For many students from underserved communities, high school might be too late or at least very late in the game to get on the path to success in college and careers. Ricardo didn't lack the intelligence to thrive academically; he lacked the tools, including self-discipline, academic perseverance, and the willingness to ask for help. If those had been introduced to him in sixth grade and continuously honed, Ricardo would be graduating on time and with honors.

Roxbury Prep could be my blank slate, an opportunity to build a curriculum and staff that wouldn't merely teach subjects and check off the boxes. Evan and I could make sure our students learned how to learn. I picked up the phone and called him. We agreed that I would handle curriculum and instruction, while

Evan took care of operations and finances. We would both work closely with students and their families.

I was twenty-four years old, and about to run a school.

Meanwhile, Teresa Rodriguez walked into my classroom one day after classes ended with even more exciting news about my future:

"I know who you're going to marry!" she announced.

CHAPTER SEVEN

TERESA'S MARRIAGE PLOT TURNED OUT TO BE A DEFT BIT OF STAGE-craft, neatly dovetailing my professional aspirations with my personal ones. Melissa Steel was one of Teresa's good friends from college, and she had just launched her own career in education, teaching first graders in Harlem. Teresa had told her all about me, and my plans to open Roxbury Prep. She said Melissa was intrigued. What she hadn't told Melissa, however, was that she was supposed to marry me.

Melissa was less than a year out of a serious breakup, and not exactly back in the dating pool, Teresa admitted. She planned on introducing me via email as a first-time principal eager to get the word out about his new charter school in order to recruit teachers and build a network of like-minded educators to share ideas and contacts. I did, in fact, want to do that, and with considerably more urgency than getting married. Teresa warned me not to come on too strong. I didn't remind her that the wedding was her idea in the first place.

One of the biggest movies the previous year had been Nora Ephron's rom-com *You've Got Mail*, starring Tom Hanks and Meg Ryan. Melissa and I scripted our own real-life version, exchanging weekly emails via Yahoo. There was something courtly yet hip about flirting in the early era of home internet. Hitting the Send button and imagining an email winging its way to someone's in-box was gratifying, and the possibility of finding Melissa's response in mine a few days later added a small rush of anticipation to my workaholic life. We would later discover that we'd both spent a lot of time crafting responses that would seem light in tone but still businesslike, with a dash of personal information. I was running my responses through Evan, which provided a welcome break from the long, hard hours we were putting in trying to get everything in place so we could open Roxbury Prep that fall. Melissa, it turned out, was sending her first drafts to herself to reread and polish. I would pick her brain with earnest questions about her take on school administration, assessing student progress, involving parents, and so forth. I'd share some funny, self-deprecating story about myself or our efforts to get the school open, then slide in a personal question or two. I learned that she was the daughter of a Ghanaian pediatrician turned public health consultant, and a white American economist at the World Bank. Her parents' careers regularly took them overseas, and Melissa and her brother had grown up citizens of the world. Born in Ghana, Melissa had spent much of her childhood in Côte d'Ivoire, with Washington DC serving as the family's US home base. Exploring the far-flung corners of the world was one of her passions.

We soon fell into a regular pattern. I would send her an email on Saturday, and she would respond on Wednesday. This went on for six weeks.

"You should meet each other!" Teresa exclaimed as if it had never dawned on her, when Melissa told her about the ongoing correspondence.

I casually mentioned in my next email that I was coming down to New York the following weekend to visit my grandmother, and asked whether Melissa might like to go grab a bite to eat sometime during my (totally contrived) trip.

We decided to meet up at the corner of the West Fourth Street subway station in Greenwich Village, which was not remotely near my grandmother's apartment in the Bronx, but that didn't matter, since my grandmother had no idea I was even in New York. I had tracked down a photo of Melissa in a professional publication, and knew she was attractive before we even began emailing. When I saw how fashion-model gorgeous she was in person, I was gripped with the fear that she was way out of my league. I guess the sense that I had very little chance of success may have made me less nervous and more open. Might as well swing for the fences. That first date lasted five hours. We ate dinner at an Italian place, then had ice cream cones in the park as we talked and talked. We finished the night listening to live music at a blues bar off Bleecker Street. Reluctant to say goodbye, we made plans to get together the next day.

This time, we decided to wander uptown. After Saturday brunch on the Upper West Side, we made our way to the Harlem Book Fair. We bonded as we talked about the books that impacted us as kids, what we liked to read as adults, and the benefits and pitfalls of the gentrification that was just beginning to emerge in Harlem. We compared our stories of growing up with mixed racial heritage in varied demographic contexts. It felt good to connect with someone who instantly understood the emotional shorthand of what it was like to walk through a door and realize you had just integrated an all-white setting, or to try to find your place in all-Black or multiracial settings. Her childhood move from Côte d'Ivoire to DC was not unlike mine from New York City to San Juan, Puerto Rico, hungering to find roots in a place you expected to feel familiar but didn't. We shared stories of sometimes feeling like we didn't quite fit in fully and other times feeling a responsibility to act as a translator or bridge builder. When it was finally time for me to head back to Boston, I asked Melissa if I could see her again. That's when she dropped what felt already like a small bombshell: She was leaving in ten days to travel across South America and would be gone for a whole month. I didn't have to think twice before promising to come back the following weekend for our next date.

The following Friday, I came back to New York for dinner and then jazz at a club near Lincoln Center. Over dinner at a Thai restaurant, Melissa laughed as I channeled a bit of my father's and Uncle Hal's flair for storytelling. I told her how profoundly influenced I had been by my summer as an intern at the US Education Department through the Truman Fellowship. I felt confident that describing my work on the Clinton administration's initiatives to strengthen the pipeline into teaching was spellbinding, but what really caught Melissa's attention was my account of a party thrown by a couple of my fellow Truman Scholars.

One of the hosts had a father who was a significant figure in the DC national security establishment (CIA, Defense Department, or something of that sort) and the family lived in a big house near the Potomac River in the Palisades, a neighborhood that was populated with the Washington political and business elite. I arrived at the tony address anticipating snacks, music, dancing, and maybe a little Trivial Pursuit—that's what you might expect from several dozen super-nerds committed to careers in public service. Imagine my surprise when I walked through the door to discover one of the co-hosts wearing a dress made of Saran wrap. That turned out to be merely the cold open of a crazy evening, which culminated with drunken wading in a stream at the edge of the property and some very short-term pairing off (in which I was not involved, but by which I was totally scandalized—and sort of still am since many of the folks would later sit alongside or opposite each other negotiating legislation in the halls of Congress or arguing cases in federal court). Melissa and I bonded over my total naivety. I began sharing some light tidbits of my personal journey, too, like living among a literal menagerie with my brother, Gil. Even though it was early in our relationship, it seemed important to get everything exactly right. I remember leaning over the table in the midst of the jazz set to ask Melissa if I could hold her hand. She giggled and took my hand. It was like I had passed her a note the way we used to at P.S. 276, saying "Do you like me?" with "Yes" and "No" boxes, and she passed the note back with a check mark next to "Yes!" I still remember how electric the moment felt, and I think about it even now when I take Melissa's hand at a show or concert.

The next day, we visited the Metropolitan Museum of Art, settling on a bench in a sculpture garden to share more of our life stories and dreams for the future. For the first time in my life, I removed all the filters, unlocked all the secret doors, and truly shared who I was and what I had endured as a child. All the dark details and survival tactics that defined those tenderest years. After I lost my parents, I was never offered counseling, and as an adult, I never sought therapy. The closest I came to analyzing my trauma, as I got older, was comparing it to the Stockdale Paradox (described in the Jim Collins book *Good to Great*, among other places), which refers to the stoicism of Vice Admiral James Stockdale, the highest-ranking American naval officer held prisoner-of-war in Vietnam. Stockdale endured over seven years of torture and solitary confinement in a windowless concrete cell. His captors shattered his shoulder, a bone in his back, and twice broke a leg. But Stockdale's spirit remained invincible. After his release, he revealed that the POWs least likely to survive were the optimists. They were the ones who believed they would be released by Christmas, and when that passed, by Easter, then Thanksgiving. The optimists, Stockdale explained, died of a broken heart. The pessimists, who lived every day believing freedom would never come, died of bitterness. Realists were the ones who prevailed, because they were able to accept the ugly truth of their situation yet never stopped believing they could survive and one day be free. By date three, I didn't want to be the stoic kid in my Brooklyn bedroom anymore. I didn't want to watch people leading the joyful, loving life I hoped for. I wanted to live it. Sitting that afternoon among the glorious giants carved from stone, we quizzed each other about every topic in the relationship catalog: kids, money, religion, exes. Finally, one or the other of us voiced out loud the obvious question we were each thinking: *So, what are we doing, do we give this a try?*

Logistically it made no sense. We lived four hours apart. Long-distance relationships always fail. And I was about to undertake the most daunting task of my life—starting and running a school. For her part, Melissa loved her students and her job working at a small, innovative New York City public school designed to focus on what the best research said about teaching children how to read. We both had full plates and big plans, but we also felt the same magnet's pull, and at the end of the day, it was too exciting to ignore. I promised to be at the airport waiting when she returned from South America.

Throughout her trip, we returned to our exchange of lengthy emails. Melissa described in beautiful detail her adventures from the volcanoes of Costa Rica to the cobblestone streets of Cartagena, where she was moved by the murals in the church of San Pedro Claver, showing the saint prostrating himself at the feet of enslaved African people, tending to the sick and dying as they disembarked from their captors' ships in chains. This, in turn, sparked a long email discussion about what faith meant to each of us. I shared the important role of the Black Catholic community in my life, particularly St. Francis de Sales in Roxbury. Although she was raised Methodist and not a churchgoer, Melissa and I quickly found common ground in our spirituality, both of us committed to service as worship. That exchange, in fact, prompted me to tell Teresa she was absolutely right. Melissa really could be the one.

Evan and I had spent all winter and spring pounding the sidewalks of Roxbury and Dorchester, posting flyers and holding informational sessions at public libraries. The goal was to recruit seventy-five potential students to enroll in the inaugural class of sixth graders we hoped to welcome to Roxbury Prep come fall. The flyers summarized our mission to set every student on the road not only to college acceptance, but college graduation. A college degree was the passport to economic independence and self-determination, and we wanted our students to have the critical thinking, the writing skills, and the study habits that would secure that future for them.

We poured our zeal and idealism onto a simple handout sheet, introducing the "3-C's"—Curriculum, Character, and Community—that formed Roxbury Prep's core values and laid the foundation for the school. Unfortunately, the flyers couldn't feature any photos of the school, classrooms, or teachers, because we hadn't gotten that far. It was like reverse engineering the Field of Dreams.

Two nerdy guys standing by city bus stops or public transit stations, eagerly trying to buttonhole parents with prepubescent kids in tow, could not have looked anything but sketchy in neighborhoods where outsiders were regarded warily, but people did, in fact, stop to listen when they heard the words "new public school."

Evan and I no doubt benefited from the unreasonable esteem bestowed on Harvard grads, but it still amazed me that anyone would entrust a couple of random strangers with zero experience running a school to get their kids into college.

On the other hand, from my work in Mission Hill, I understood why parents would grasp at a chance to put their kids on a better trajectory. In Roxbury, only 9 percent of the adults had bachelor's degrees and many of the neighborhood district schools were struggling with significant discipline issues, painfully low English and math proficiency rates, and chronic absenteeism. The demographics in Boston's high-needs neighborhoods were weighted heavily toward single mothers, and since we were seeking just sixth graders to start, many of those moms tended to be young themselves—not much older than we were. They were the short-changed alumni of the same underperforming public schools their own children were now stuck in. They wanted something better for their kids and sensed that it couldn't get any worse. We were as good a bet as any.

No one laughed in our faces when we boasted that our curriculum would make Roxbury's students competitive with their privileged peers at the city's most elite private schools or neighboring suburban districts. As a tuition-free public charter school, we insisted that we could provide all the opportunities, tools, encouragement, structure, and support they would need to thrive as they furthered their education after leaving Roxbury Prep. We promised excellent teachers, plus a well-rounded curriculum that would provide essential skills in math and reading along with broad exposure to social studies and science, field trips and cultural outings. We would hold regular town hall meetings with the parents. We promised to feed everyone breakfast and lunch, and to staff a homework and tutoring club after school and even on Saturdays.

In short, we promised to care intensely.

The kids we encountered seemed excited, too, though the longer school day sparked a few moans. Classes would run until 4:00 p.m.—two hours later than regular district school schedules across Boston. When I approached Chynah Tyler and her mom with a flyer at the Dudley Square bus station, Chynah was initially skeptical about leaving her friends, who would be going to their neighborhood middle school. But even as she hung back, I could see out of the corner of my eye how closely she was listening to all the questions her mother was asking, and how excited she was by the answers she got—not only about academic standards, but about the safe school climate we would provide, defined by uniforms and high behavioral expectations. Neither mother nor daughter mentioned at the time that Chynah had recently lost a brother to gun violence.

As the dog days of summer bore down on us, Evan and I scrambled to get the final pieces in place. Our charter promised strong academic results in exchange for greater autonomy, laying out the core elements of the program we would deliver and guaranteeing us per student funding from the state at a level approaching the local district's. We were on the hook to find a space and raise money for any renovations. One of Mission Hill's important community institutions, the Edgar P. Benjamin Healthcare Center nursing home—aka "the Benjamin"—came to the rescue on the real estate front, offering us space on the top floor to use for classrooms and offices.

As opening day grew closer, we toggled between all the educational preparations and overseeing final renovations at the nursing home—painting, arranging desks, setting up white boards, and installing lockers.

We were flooded with hundreds of applications for the six teaching slots we had to fill, and the search for the best candidates proved interesting. Our style of job interviewing caught more than a few by surprise. The charter guaranteed salaries comparable to what the Boston Public School District paid, but we weren't accountable to any bureaucracy, and there was no human resources czar to make us abide by a prefab box-checking formula. We got to make our own rules. If you were invited to interview with us, you needed to set aside a couple of hours, and it wasn't for paperwork. We put our faith more heavily in show than tell. After cross-examining applicants with questions like tag-team debate moderators in an effort to determine whether they were a good fit, Evan and I would ask them to role-play a mock lesson. We played the part of students.

Later, once we were actually open, sample lessons became an essential part of the hiring process—and I was always struck by how perceptive and insightful our students were about their "guest" teachers when we asked for their feedback. A seventh grader won't hold back if asked for an honest opinion about how boring you were. A sixth grader frustrated by dividing fractions will be thrilled if you can deliver a "light bulb" moment and help them over a hurdle. The fact that we sought the students' opinions, put trust in their radar, and acknowledged their reasoning reinforced the sense of solidarity Roxbury Prep aspired to. We were the adults in charge, but we were all in this quest for scholarship together.

Just as we had far more teacher applications than slots, we also had far more children applying than spaces available in that inaugural class.

We held a lottery and admitted eighty students. With our newly hired faculty members (including Teresa), we were able to begin holding orientation sessions in June. We walked parents and students through the structure of the day, the code of conduct, and the uniform specifics, while continuously reinforcing our constant mantra of preparation for college success. The Ten Creeds that formed the core values of Roxbury Prep were:

1. **Scholarship**: We think critically and aspire to and achieve academic excellence.
2. **Integrity**: We are honest and ethical in our words and our actions.

3. **Dignity**: We have self-respect and honor our heritages.
4. **Responsibility**: We are accountable for our decisions and our actions.
5. **Perseverance**: We are resourceful, work hard, and always strive to do our best.
6. **Community**: We use our talents to make positive contributions to our communities.
7. **Leadership**: We act on the principle that if we are not part of the solution, we are part of the problem.
8. **Peace**: We resolve conflicts with compassion and help others to do the same.
9. **Social Justice**: We endeavor to make our society more just.
10. **Investment**: We are reflective, act with foresight, and invest in our futures.

Toward the middle of July, our teachers began working full-time, developing the curriculum for the year. Guided by the Massachusetts state standards (then regarded as some of the best in the country), we determined in painstaking detail exactly what students would read, what essay topics they would research and write about, what math problem sets they would tackle, what science experiments they would conduct, and what historical simulations they would engage in. Unlike my first year of teaching, where the first day began with nothing more than a textbook and good wishes, we wanted our teachers to have a thorough plan for the year and we invested in creating the time, space, and support.

With the teachers, Evan and I walked through a minute-by-minute tick tock of the school day—who would greet students at the buses and at the door, who would stand where during hallway transitions, etc. We went over it multiple times. Evan and I wanted it to be perfect. In August 1999, Roxbury Prep opened its doors, and the show began.

I instilled the wisdom of Harry Streep in my new staff, urging them to plan their lessons with a focus on what the students would do during that class, to maximize not just the rigor of the curriculum, but the level of student engagement in hands-on learning. As a result, our kids would be dissecting a squid, building models of atoms out of breakfast cereal, and calculating energy by sending marbles rocketing down the tracks of miniature roller coasters made out of pipe insulation. In social studies, Athens and Sparta would face off in a debate to determine which city-state was superior. We were off to a good start.

Through our doors would walk kids like Kenny, so smart, talented, and exuberant. "I have ARRIVED!" he declared with a grand flourish, not just his first day, but frequently throughout his middle school career, whether he was straggling into class tardy again or boarding the bus for a field trip. Kenny was one of those boys who often got into trouble for misbehaving, but it was as if he was always kind of winking at you as he acted up.

His mother was earnest and involved, but Kenny, with no dad at home, was beginning to gravitate toward a worrisome group of older boys who hung out in his neighborhood. Kenny's younger sister, Shakeema, would also attend Roxbury Prep, a quiet and studious girl. Her brother, though, yearned to be seen, heard, and celebrated. Kenny was the school clown, a skilled rapper, a popular kid with charm to spare. When we took the kids to the roller rink, we were all surprised to hear Kenny's voice suddenly come booming over the sound system. He had somehow persuaded the house DJ into turning over the microphone. The kids cheered proudly as Kenny emceed. His teachers and I would worry about him, and cheer for him, long after he graduated from Roxbury Prep.

Then there was the girl I will call Linda, the lost girl. She was a loner who had conflicts with teachers and classmates. She didn't seem to have many friends and scared away the ones who tried. Linda wasn't mean—just volatile and angry. If a kid accidentally bumped into her in the hall, she'd yell and curse, accusing them of doing it on purpose. If a teacher asked what was wrong, she would ask why they were picking on her. There was a pattern to her moods: Mondays were really hard for her. Tuesdays were good. Wednesdays were very good. Thursdays were okay. Fridays were a mess. Her mother was erratic when we tried to contact her. We suspected addiction and debated whether to involve social services. But we had no proof, and what would happen to Linda then? How would a scary and notoriously broken foster care system save her? We needed to find a way to draw her closer, not push her away, much as Uncle Hal and Aunt Jean had done with me when I was so sullen and angry after Andover. Before we could finalize a plan, Linda and her mother were gone, moving away without a word.

There were dozens of kids we would come to know like Chynah, whom I had first met while handing out flyers at the bus station. Chynah was serious and well behaved most of the time, but reluctant to engage as she tried to size up her new school and where she fit in. I remembered that yearning to belong all too well from my own childhood. Besides the education it would provide, I wanted Roxbury Prep to become a special place every child would come to think of as their own. Chynah would later describe Roxbury Prep as the community that nurtured her not only as a student, but as a leader, when running successfully for a seat in the Massachusetts state legislature.

There were puzzles for us to solve, as well, like Chris, who somehow had been promoted to sixth grade even though he couldn't read. Chris was smart and affable, and we discovered that he had used his keen memory to mask his inability to read, carefully remembering what the teacher had said aloud to parrot back later, until Roxbury Prep's high expectations caught up with him. Unable to complete the work that was expected of him, Chris started to get in trouble. Fortunately, we got to the root of it quickly, and found him an Orton-Gillingham tutor trained to use an intensive phonics program to help dyslexic students get on track. Orton-Gillingham worked and Chris would later go on to serve honorably in the military and to become an entrepreneur.

And there were the high achievers like Titciana, a shy girl who just needed the encouragement and validation to become the leader all her teachers knew she could be. With mentoring from her sixth grade math teacher, she would go on to found Roxbury Prep's math peer-tutoring program, mobilizing other strong students to help struggling peers. If Roxbury Prep's method worked the way we hoped, the academically gifted kids would never grow bored or complacent, and the uncertain ones would be brimming with confidence by the time we sent them off to high school. Years later, Titciana would be back in the same classroom as a math teacher herself and ultimately become Roxbury Prep's principal.

Opening Roxbury Prep wasn't my only reason to celebrate that summer. Melissa had returned from her South America trip. I was waiting with flowers at the airport. When our eyes met, she brightened into a huge smile.

We plunged into the new chapter of our lives, determined to prove the naysayers wrong about the viability of long-distance relationships. My job demanded attention long after the final bell rang at school. Teachers were required to submit their lesson plans for the following week on Thursday, and I would spend Friday and often part of Saturday religiously poring over each one and offering detailed feedback. I hoped to give the teachers the same clarity and kindness that Harry Streep had once shown me. I wanted every class to deliver the zeal I had experienced with Mr. Osterweil and Miss D. I wanted students to be the ones doing the "academic sweating," with fewer multiple-choice answers to guess at and circle, and more open-ended questions requiring thoughtful, written responses.

We didn't want to evaluate how well an English class comprehended literature through rote regurgitation of the plot, text, and characters. The students had to analyze the choices an author made. We sought active engagement over silent reading in social studies class, helping the kids dive into preparation for a mock trial, or plot Paul Revere's midnight ride with the dangers and enemies he might face along the way.

Melissa was busy with her second year of teaching in Harlem, but had flexibility with her schedule, and assumed most of the burden of commuting in our relationship, taking the four-hour Peter Pan bus from New York City to Boston for our weekends together. We went apple picking that autumn and skiing in the winter. The latter, like many of our dates, was a Roxbury Prep field trip. A Bobby McFerrin concert at Symphony Hall, a play at the Huntington Theater, and a Red Sox game at Fenway Park were group dates with a busload of tweens. In fact, Melissa was a regular on Saturday night Roxbury Prep outings with kids, teachers, and parents—at first as a "teacher friend" just coming along for the fun, and eventually as Mr. King's "girlfriend," which generated lots of predictable middle school curiosity and giggles.

I became a self-taught travel agent specializing in budget deals for some romantic getaways minus the peanut gallery, planning escapes to Italy and Mexico. Melissa went on a mission to make me loosen up with dates I wouldn't have planned on my own, like the guided-tour Rome bar-crawl that started with an entire jug of wine, and continued with delightful banter about sports over cheese and more wine with our tour mates from Columbus, Ohio, and then ended with me unceremoniously rolling down the window of the cab back to the hotel to throw up. We got the free cruise to Tulum, Mexico, by signing up to listen to a time-share pitch, convinced we could withstand the pressure to buy in. The only reason we escaped signing on the dotted line was because our ship was about to depart and the onshore realty office where we were being vacation-brainwashed couldn't talk as fast as we could sprint.

We also made the rounds of family introductions.

I first met Melissa's parents at Thanksgiving in Washington DC. A few of their international friends were also invited. I was wowed by the broad discussion topics over the dinner table, where conversation hopscotched from music and theater to economic development in Sub-Saharan Africa to American domestic

politics to the best restaurants to go to in London. It was sometimes hard to keep up, but I loved the challenge.

Suffice it to say that Melissa's meet-the-family experience was
less cosmopolitan. Melissa met the whole King clan at once when
she joined me in Northern California for a family reunion at my
cousin Hal's house in San Rafael. It was a boisterous gathering,
reminiscent of the backyard parties at Uncle Hal and Aunt Jean's
Cherry Hill house. Melissa's induction featured lots of tall tales,
laughter, and good-natured teasing, plus an unfortunate argument between Cousin Hal and Cousin Dwight about who had
a bigger didgeridoo (a large wind instrument they had bought
as souvenirs from their respective trips to Australia). There were
also cutthroat matches of UNO and Pictionary, where it didn't
really matter if your drawing made any sense as long as you could
out-argue any challengers. The happiness and love I felt that
night made me realize that I was no longer mentally gazing out
my Brooklyn window. Everything I needed to create the family
I wanted was inside, now.

In May, I visited Melissa's parents again, this time secretly. In
Adwoa Steel's native Ghana, I had learned, there was a tradition akin to an engagement ceremony among the Ashanti people,
where the suitor's family performs a "knocking ceremony" at the
prospective bride's family home, to ask permission for their son
to marry the other family's daughter. If the answer is yes, the two
sides then jovially barter over a dowry, and gifts are exchanged.
I called the Steels and invited them to lunch. The Ashanti is
a matriarchal society, and I flew to DC hoping to impress my
would-be mother-in-law with my cultural awareness. At a hotel
rooftop restaurant overlooking the White House, the three of
us made polite small talk, and our meal came. I couldn't get up

my nerve to state my business, and finally, as the awkwardness stretched on with dessert menus in hand, Melissa's father, Biff, blurted out: "I assume you didn't fly here to take us out to lunch. Is there anything you want to say?"

I explained how much I loved their daughter, and that I had come to ask for their blessing for my plan to propose to Melissa. I promised to give her the best life I could. They graciously gave me their blessing, and I swore them to secrecy.

Once I had that taken care of, I just needed to figure out how to set the stage to get Melissa to say yes, too. We had talked about marriage, of course, and we had even done that casual-but-not-really jewelry store browsing that couples in love do. I had saved up enough to buy the ring Melissa had admired the most. I then turned to Eric, a trustworthy romantic, to help me plot the details of my proposal.

Finally, I called Melissa and casually mentioned that I was bringing a vanload of Roxbury Prep kids to the Metropolitan Museum of Art that weekend. She was used to the group dates with background debates over the best X-Men superpower or Britney Spears song. I suggested it would be easier for her to ride back up to Boston in the van with us than to take her usual bus trip up to Boston for the weekend. That she didn't challenge logic with such a flawed premise in the first place is a testament to her good nature.

When I showed up at the museum and went to greet her, Melissa demurely shook off my hand when I tried to take hers and glanced around, worried that some kids might see us. We were always hypervigilant about no PDA around them. "Oh, it's okay," I insisted. "They're in another room." I led her to the European Sculpture Court, where sunlight from huge windows illuminated the marble masterpieces looking down on us. We sat on a bench, and I pulled out a scrapbook I had made of our emails, and a photo album of our dates, field trips, and adventures. I reminded her of what I had confided to her not long after we met.

"Every other relationship I've ever had, I could anticipate at the beginning what might make it end," I reiterated, "but I couldn't do that with us." I pulled out the ring and asked her to marry me.

She said yes; we kissed and held each other close. After a couple minutes, Melissa broke from my hug and asked anxiously when we needed to meet the kids. She was relieved to learn that the field trip was just a ruse and that rather than a four-hour post-engagement van ride to Boston with middle schoolers, our next stop was a cute bed-and-breakfast in Rehoboth Beach, Delaware, a favorite vacation spot of hers growing up.

We had a whole weekend just to ourselves before the school bell rang again.

CHAPTER EIGHT

As Roxbury Prep headed toward its second year, we were excited not only by the academic progress we could already see the kids making, but by the deepening bond that was taking hold among the students, the faculty, the parents, and the neighborhood.

We gave the same thought to building a sense of community that we did to fine-tuning the curriculum. In addition to regular school assemblies each week, we hosted a December Kwanzaa celebration and extraordinarily well-attended monthly family nights, where we provided meals and childcare to make it just a little easier for parents to participate, especially single working moms juggling so much. But something, we felt, was still lacking, and that something was crucial to our success: "the J-factor."

Joy. We needed to infuse more joy into each school day.

The kids, after all, had been thrown into an entirely new culture of learning, where the days were longer, the work was harder, and the expectations were higher. Their neighborhood friends didn't have to wear uniforms or do as much homework—if any at all. They didn't have rules against talking in the hallway between periods, which was essential, given the tight space and narrow hallways at the Benjamin and our desire to maximize instructional time. Their teachers or principal didn't call their parents if there were missing assignments or a detention on the horizon because of classroom antics.

Maybe it sounds like a lame oxymoron, but I took happiness seriously. I didn't merely believe it mattered in ensuring that students thrived—I was certain it did. I wanted every child at Roxbury Prep to feel what I had at their age—to love school, and to love learning. The classrooms of my own childhood had become my North Star as an educator and administrator, and when I reflected on what it was that made Mr. Osterweil and Miss D so impactful—what special gift they brought to the children they taught—the words that always came to mind were "rigor and joy."

Securing a charter in the first place had been a grueling and highly competitive process, but we were hardly home free. The cost of our autonomy, the freedom to adopt our own core mission and teaching style, came with an ultimatum to show good results—enrollment, a waitlist, strong academic outcomes in test scores and student success after graduation, parent and community enthusiasm—within five years or lose it all.

We doubled in size that second year, with a new class of incoming sixth graders replacing the ones now entering seventh grade. In another year, we would be grades 6 through 8, a full-on middle school. Whether we would keep growing to add on a high school was still under debate. For the time being, though, we needed to recruit six new teachers, which would bring our faculty to a grand total of twelve.

Evan is the one who gets credit for Jabali Sawicki. The two had met when Jabali was working as a junior teacher in the Summerbridge program at Kentucky Country Day, in Louisville, Kentucky. Summerbridge (now called Breakthrough Collaborative) provided academic enrichment programs for middle school students from historically underserved communities on the campuses of selective private high schools. In addition to demanding academics and fun extracurricular activities, students had the opportunity to get comfortable being on a selective campus where they were often chronically underrepresented.

As a child of color in a gifted program, raised in middle-class neighborhoods, I had felt miserably out of place at Andover. Maybe the taste of acclimatization that programs like Summerbridge provided would have helped me feel more a part of than apart from the elite prep school culture.

At Summerbridge, classrooms were staffed by teachers (often from the private school) and high-school-age junior teachers. Jabali, who grew up in the Bay Area with a single mom who worked at the post office, had made his way to Louisville for the summer, and Evan, then teaching at Kentucky Country Day, was the program director.

When I met him, Jabali had just graduated from Oberlin, where he studied philosophy and biology. We hired him to teach science, and the J-factor skyrocketed as soon as he stepped through the door.

Jabali was joy personified, one of those people who could bring fun to a root canal. One of his first lessons involved converting his classroom into a colorful replica of a giant cell.

Students would migrate from the nucleus to the membrane to the cytoplasm for different activities and lessons. And Jabali was just getting started.

He also had a talent for performing and was soon turning dense textbook explanations into catchy songs. He could rap about laboratory tools or change the lyrics of a hit by Destiny's Child to create an earworm so the kids would remember the steps of photosynthesis. His lesson plans included tons of experiments for the kids to conduct. His classes were usually bubbling with laughter, song, and any number of illustrative laboratory concoctions. Outside the classroom, Jabali fully embraced his de facto role as Roxbury Prep's ambassador of fun by helping to organize our trips to cultural and sports events, which students and often their families were able to attend cost-free or for a minimal price thanks to blocks of tickets offered by our donors or paid for from funds we kept on hand for cultural enrichment.

Rewards, prizes, and recognition were an important part of our school culture. Kids who made the honor roll were treated to a big trip, like skiing, each grading period. Others collected "Creed Deeds," our form of fake currency for teachers that we invented in our second year thanks to Jabali's encouragement to balance out our demerit system. The Creed Deeds recognized positive behavior that reflected one of the school's ten creeds. A teacher might reward a student for staying after school to help clean up after a science lab or for being a good friend to a classmate having a bad day. At the end of the grading period, students could turn those Creed Deeds into rewards like a gift certificate to Barnes & Noble or passes to the aquarium. The student with the most Creed Deeds usually chose "Co-Director Service," which made them an honorary administrator. The "co-director" got to be treated like royalty for a day, with Evan and me carrying their books from class to class, cleaning off their desks, and serving carry-out food for lunch, which we would all eat in my office. But there was one award even more coveted than French fries with the school directors or tickets to a ball game, one that wasn't for sale: The Spirit Stick.

The Spirit Stick was a bedazzled wand with a tassel on top, which Jabali had created to bestow on the student deemed to have done the most stellar job of exhibiting Roxbury Prep's core values in a given week. Teachers and staff would huddle to compare notes beforehand to determine the winner—it could be someone who pulled a C-minus up to an A in spelling or a rambunctious student like Kenny working so intently on focusing that they were demerit-free for the first time all semester. We might single out a math whiz who showed leadership and kindness as a peer tutor, or a budding artist who spent hours creating a beautiful collage depicting ancient Egypt for social studies.

Passing the baton to a new Spirit Stick winner was the grand finale of our regular Friday "community meeting," and the ceremony never grew old. The rollicking assembly was a tradition we initiated to build school pride and solidarity at Roxbury Prep, a fun way to wrap up the week with a summer-camp-like program of songs, contests, games, awards, and entertainment. Presentations ranged from readings of students' original poetry or other creative writing to reflections on the week from the co-directors or teachers, who usually told engaging stories and pointed lessons echoing the style of Sunday church sermons. The assembly's grand finale was an always-hilarious skit starring students and teachers, written by Jabali and often inspired by a popular television show or movie. The skit was riddled with clues about the mystery student about to win the Spirit Stick, the script dropping hints about what that deserving pupil had done and who it might be. Sound effects and snippets from contemporary songs playing on Jabali's huge boom box helped build the suspense.

Knowing that most of our kids might never before have experienced being singled out as "the best" in their old schools and seeing them bask in attention motivated us even more to keep pushing them to realize the potential that our ever-climbing test scores and classroom assessments confirmed was there. We could see our kids rise to the challenges we put before them. They bought into pleasing even the toughest teacher, Catalina Sáenz.

She was the only Latina in the math department at Wellesley as an undergrad and brought youthful zeal to a subject that so many students dreaded. Math was about procedures and problem solving, rules and application—but it was Catalina's classroom culture that helped her students thrive. She was strict but warm, with very high expectations. "You should know your times tables like you know your name," she told her students. They knew she was a tough grader, a cold caller in the classroom, that she would phone your mom and send you home with extra work if you needed it. The students also knew that Catalina would tutor anyone who asked for help after school or during lunch. Ms. Saenz was the teacher who helped Titciana launch the math peer-tutoring program. Like Mr. Osterweil and Miss D, Catalina asked a lot of her students, but also provided love, encouragement, and joy. Even the kids at the bottom of her class were eager to earn her approval, which was a powerful motivator.

Roxbury Prep's teachers as a whole were inspired by the freedom and the support they had to push boundaries and find creative ways to approach the curriculum. It's not hard to imagine the resistance a teacher at a traditional middle school would have met if, like Josh Phillips, they asked their principal for permission to take the entire sixth grade on field trips to visit a synagogue, a mosque, and a Christian church for a unit on world religions. My response was quick: Great idea!

There was no such thing as "stay in your lane" among our young, visionary team. One day, Josh came to Evan and me with another idea. "The kids need athletics," he said. "A lot of them want to play soccer and basketball." Physical ed at the time consisted of taking classes to the park across the street from the nursing home to use blacktops and playing fields. In bad weather, the nursing home let us use a community room for indoor PE. Evan and I told Josh to write up a proposal for an actual athletics program. He didn't object that spreadsheets and cost analysis were outside the purview of a twenty-six-year-old history teacher— he just set off to do his research and came back with a detailed breakdown of what equipment and uniforms would cost, what facilities were available, and a list of other charters he'd called who were interested in forming a league. A couple of years later, Roxbury Prep won the Charter Cup, but our athletics program represented an even bigger win by our measure. A teacher had shown the kids by example how to put in the effort and turn an idea into reality.

Ricardo, my former high school pupil on the brink of flunking out, had been absolutely right. Teaching kids how to learn at *this* age was empowering them at the right moment. What we were doing in middle school would stop the snowball effect of falling hopelessly behind. It would spare these students the defeat and demoralization that turned so many urban public high schools into dropout factories. We were jubilant when we began seeing reading, math, and language skills going up to grade level, and we kept pushing once we did. The mountain to climb to earn a college degree, support a family, and claim the American dream wasn't getting any lower in an America struggling with ever greater income inequality, especially for kids of color from low-income backgrounds. There was no such thing as providing a child too many tools for success.

Our reward system sought to make academic achievement as cool as "mad skills" on a basketball court or soccer field, and the Spirit Stick was our equivalent of an MVP award. The student body erupted in wild cheers, whoops, and applause each time a new honoree was announced at the end of Jabali's skits. I never could have imagined how validated I felt by that weekly pandemonium.

I'd come a long way since my earliest attempts at community building at the Mission Hill summer camp Eric and I ran, where I considered myself—at nineteen—the designated bringer-of-structure (which would by default make Eric, not unfittingly, the agent of chaos). My Waterloo came one evening when Eric and I thought a piñata seemed like a grand idea to surprise the Mission Hill campers and their families at an evening academic celebration. We had everyone gathered in a big room (little siblings, too), and it took nanoseconds for the "Little League ringers" in the group to smash the piñata to smithereens. Candy came flying out, and all of the kids (toddlers included) flung themselves at once into the sugary debris field, forming a giant screaming scrum. Everyone was trying to grab as many Skittles and Nerds as possible. It was a totally natural response—100 percent predictable—and the scene would probably make a hilarious viral video today. But I was utterly mortified. I had an overwhelming sense of being out of control, and I just froze. A counselor hurled herself bodily on top of the scrum to restore some order while I stood there in silent, helpless panic. Now I oversaw twice as many kids making twice as much noise every Friday, and I reveled in the sweet commotion.

At Roxbury Prep, my home life was benefiting from an enhanced J-factor, too. I had spent the summer of 2000 starting my doctorate in education back at Teachers College, living with Melissa in her Fort Greene apartment, and enjoying the city as a young couple in love. Just going for a walk offered a boundless variety of free entertainment in New York City: You could watch break dancers challenge each other with dazzling moves on one corner and listen to a quartet of Juilliard students perform a Bach fugue on the next.

In Boston, our social circle was a tapestry of old friends, like Eric and Teresa (who had become Roxbury Prep's reading teacher) and new ones—a small universe of young educators forever brainstorming over ways to deliver on America's unfulfilled promise of a free and equitable public education for every child. Happy hours were a way for us to vent and dream. Melissa also had a wonderful crew of New York City friends deeply engaged in civic life: the health care policy expert married to the housing expert; the early career politico engaged to the journalist. I loved our debates over dinners sampling the world's cuisine at New York City's endless supply of restaurants—I could eat my way from Senegal to Scandinavia as we uncovered the city's hidden gems in little pocket neighborhoods. The only fare that was off limits was street food, an artifact of Melissa being the daughter of a public health expert.

At the end of the summer, Melissa moved in with me back to my third-floor walk-up bachelor pad in Jamaica Plain and began teaching kindergarten at another high-performing Boston charter school. We were both working hard, often doing paperwork side by side on the sofa or at a favorite coffee shop—me reviewing lesson plans, Melissa writing them. Sundays, though, always belonged to us. Melissa and I would go to Mass together at St. Francis de Sales, the church adjacent to public housing in Roxbury. St. Francis had a congregation largely of color and fully embraced the Black Catholic spiritual tradition. There was gospel singing and traditional call-and-response during the homily with the priest, both more typical of Black Baptist churches. The pastor, Father Tom, was a white Irish Catholic and a Jesuit, who was so devoted to the culture of his congregation that he had gotten a degree in Black Catholic theology and tradition at Xavier University, a historically Black university in New Orleans. He always delivered a great homily, which would spark a deep discussion for Melissa and me on the way home. After church, Melissa and I would head to a favorite health food market in downtown Jamaica Plain to get sandwiches, BBQ sweet potato chips, and lemonade to bring back home for a couch picnic. Even more important than the intellectual discussions I enjoyed with Melissa was the lightness she brought to my life. Melissa and I could be silly together, from watching absurdly campy dating shows to laughing about the antics of her kindergarteners or my sixth and seventh graders. For the first time in memory, I could feel what it was like to live in an emotional space where the fight-or-flight switch didn't have to be within reach. There was an ease with Melissa, an assurance that I could lose my footing, or simply dare to let go, and her love would always be the safety net beneath me.

A few weeks before our wedding, my grandmother collapsed while out shopping for a dress to wear for the big occasion. A cousin called me from the hospital: She was gone. Melissa and I had just visited her in the Bronx. Her social life for decades had revolved around a community center where she regularly played bingo; its recent closure had shrunk her world considerably, and I knew that had taken a toll on her quality of life. But she had been a healthy eighty-four-year-old who made us arroz con pollo, rellenos, and maduros the afternoon we last saw her. I had been looking forward to sharing the happiest day of my life with her. Burying her instead was a shock. My heart ached for both my grandmother and my mother on my wedding day, not just for my loss but for what they had both missed, the chance to see me so happy and filled with hope.

Some two hundred guests traveled to the church Melissa and I had chosen for our ceremony on May 27, 2001, in Rockport, Massachusetts, on a rugged New England shore not far from Gloucester. Father Tom officiated, and a gospel choir called Confirmation sang throughout the ceremony, including one of my favorite hymns, "I've Got a Testimony," which features the line "As I look back over my life and I think things over, I can truly say that I've been blessed, I've got a testimony." Melissa wore a vintage satin dress passed down over a hundred years among the women on her father's side of the family, with each bride's name sewn into the waistband. Melissa's was the fifth. We jumped the broom after being pronounced husband and wife.

We danced our first dance to Stevie Wonder's lush "Ribbon in the Sky." We presented guests with traditional Ghanaian gifts of kente cloth that Melissa's parents had brought back for us from a trip to Africa. The narrow strips of brightly colored silk and cotton yarn woven by hand were traditionally stitched together to dress Ashanti royalty. Each color and distinctive kente pattern (variations of a basket weave) symbolizes something specific. Green, for example, conveys land, vegetation, spiritual growth, and renewal, while a certain pattern might symbolize forgiveness, tolerance, and fairness. A garment can tell an entire story to a keen kente reader.

Despite the fun, high-energy vibe, I found myself carefully tracking how much my brother, Gil, was drinking. I wanted to believe that everything would be fine, but I couldn't let go of the last remnants of my teenage hypervigilance and worry that Gil would erupt at any moment in some irrational rage.

Dinner had just been served when I heard a disturbance at the table behind us. Gil's voice rose loudly above the room's convivial hum. He was berating a server who had failed to bring him hot sauce. She was apologizing profusely that there was none. Gil demanded to know how that was possible, launching into a loud rant about hot sauce being the world's most popular condiment. I was instantly fourteen again, as though I was walking on eggshells back at Hiawatha Lane, willing myself to become invisible, out of the line of my brother's fire. I put my fork down, remained silent, instinct commanding me not to engage. The reception carried on around me.

Fortunately, guests at Gil's table were able to quickly defuse the situation. When the family toasts started and the Kings got going, they went a little long—but my spirit was lifted by their immense love for me. Even Gil's familiar antics couldn't disrupt my joy. Remembering the isolation of Brooklyn, I felt profoundly blessed by the embrace of family and friends.

At one point while Melissa and I were dancing, I spotted Uncle Hal, Jan, and a few others huddled over Aunt Jean and helping her out. The family matriarch was in her late seventies, and the long party must have taken its toll. I'd been surprised by how frail she looked when I had first greeted her. She and Uncle Hal were still as active as ever down in Florida—they were just about to set off on another one of their frequent cruises.

I called to check on Aunt Jean the next morning before Melissa and I headed off on our honeymoon to Marbella, Spain, and was assured that it was just a bad stomachache, probably too much rich food, nothing to worry about.

By the time we came back, Aunt Jean was undergoing tests. Within a couple of weeks, doctors had a diagnosis: pancreatic cancer.

We spoke regularly on the phone, and that October, when I went down to Florida to see her, she was bedridden but lucid. Even if I wasn't ready to face it, she knew it would be the last time we saw each other. Aunt Jean always began any conversation with the same loving preamble. "How are you doing? How is Melissa?" She would make her way through the list of my professional and personal contacts, genuinely interested in news about each. "How is Evan? How about Eric? And Teresa? Is Gil doing any better?"

This time, once the ritual was complete, Aunt Jean told me how glad she was that I had found Melissa, how happy it made her to know I would be able to have the family I always wanted. I tried to express my gratitude for all she and Uncle Hal had done for me by taking me in after I got kicked out of Andover and helping me get my life on track. I talked about how the loving warmth of their household, the reliable consistency of the day-to-day routines, and the home-cooked meals gave me space to heal. "That's what family does," she said. She wanted me to know how much she loved me. And there was something else, too: "I'm proud of you."

Her words not only made me feel her love, care, and validation, but carried with them echoes of my mother and my grandmother. In the room I tried to contain my tears, but when I closed the door behind me so she could rest, I sobbed at the thought of losing her.

We spoke by phone a couple of times after that visit, but she was fading fast. When she left us, on November 7, 2001, at the age of seventy-nine, Aunt Jean was eulogized as a world traveler and ocean cruiser, a proud military wife and loving homemaker, a talented quilter, a spectacular mother, a great friend, a superb hostess with a keen sense of humor. The obituary counted five children, not four, and I was remembered as a son.

In her final months, she had made each of us a blanket to remember her by, and mine came with a second, smaller one, for the baby she was certain Melissa and I would have one day.

A lot changed that fall of 2001. Melissa had started the doctoral program at Harvard's Graduate School of Education, pursuing an EdD in human development and psychology. I was making progress toward my doctorate while still leading Roxbury Prep. The story of Roxbury Prep and how we set about fulfilling the promises of our charter actually became a part of my dissertation at Columbia.

Evan decided to leave Roxbury Prep at the end of our third year to attend law school, hoping to find a path into policy or maybe politics. Josh Phillips was named my new co-director. Life, inside and outside the school's walls, was sailing on, the waters felt smooth and predictable. Until Melissa and I discovered we were expecting.

I was beyond excited to be starting my own family at last, and beyond blessed to have in-laws whose selfless love would further those bonds I always imagined creating with a wife and children.

In Ashanti culture, "family" is a word without modifiers like nuclear or extended. Cousins are cousins, never distant ones. Mothers are all the mothers, and children are everyone's to look after, teach, and love—parameters inherent in traditional life for generations and cherished still. Melissa's parents rented an apartment a floor above ours. Her mother would be on hand to help throughout her pregnancy and after the baby was born. Her love, wisdom, and kindness greatly eased my anxiety, as well. Both Melissa and I were cool-headed and calm when she went into labor.

Actually, I was a little less calm, maybe, but that was because my beloved Yankees were in the final game of their epic 2003 playoff showdown with their arch-nemesis, the Boston Red Sox. Melissa was pacing, focused on walking and breathing to try to ease her labor pains. The baseball game had gone into extra innings, and there wasn't much I could do at that point. For the Yankees or Melissa. I rubbed Melissa's back while keeping an eye on the TV screen. In the bottom of the 11th inning, Aaron Boone hit a walk-off home run off Tim Wakefield to win the American League pennant for the Yankees. We drove to Brigham and Women's Hospital the next morning. People all over Boston were dejected—the Sox had not won a World Series since 1918 and Boston fans *hated* New York—but I was on cloud nine. We were having a baby and the Yankees won. Life didn't get any better.

Amina Adalinda Effie King came early that afternoon, healthy, beautiful, and very much beloved.

With a loving, doting grandmother at home, Melissa and I didn't have to miss a beat in our careers. Melissa's parents pivoted graciously to accommodate our growing clan, buying the top two floors in a triplex in Jamaica Plain; we lived on the third floor, with the Steels just below us.

Roxbury Prep by then was the highest-performing open-admission urban middle school in Massachusetts. Analyzing the school's evolution for my dissertation stirred my long-held ambitions to meld practice with policy to make meaningful differences in public education on a bigger scale. Recalling my summer interning at the US Department of Education and the number of policymakers I encountered there who happened to be lawyers, I decided in the fall of 2003 that my next logical career step was to apply to law school. I was grateful when both Harvard and Yale accepted me. I was tempted to go to Harvard Law School, given what a wonderful undergraduate experience I had, but after much agonizing, I elected to go to Yale. It was a smaller community with a long tradition of launching impactful careers in public service. Adwoa was crucial to the operation at hand: We all decided that it made the most sense for me to rent a small apartment in New Haven. I'd be in Connecticut Monday through Thursday, then return to Jamaica Plain to spend Friday through Sunday with the family. It was hard to be away from Melissa and Amina for days at a time, but we tried to make the most of what we had. Melissa would make the trip to New Haven with the baby whenever she could, too.

My first summer in law school, I worked in Boston for the extraordinary general counsel of the Massachusetts Department of Elementary and Secondary Education, Rhoda Schneider. She was a phenomenal lawyer with decades of experience in the role and more than one stint as acting commissioner under her belt. Her job was the dream job I had written about not just in my law school applications, but in my Truman Scholarship application back in college—the perfect intersection of lawyering and education policy.

The highlight of my stint in Rhoda's office was working alongside the lawyer defending the department's decision to revoke the charter of a struggling school that had failed to live up to its promises to outperform the local district schools and prepare students for college success. The administrative hearing had all the elements of a trial—painstaking witness prep with the department's experts, intense questioning of the witnesses, compelling documents placed into evidence. It was like having a supporting role in *Law and Order: Policy Wonk Unit*.

Much as I enjoyed the work and admired Rhoda, I concluded that her job was too much about telling the policymakers the parameters for their decisions and not enough about the actual decision making. I yearned for a role where I could make the decisions necessary each day to help more students succeed at scale—especially ones with the deck stacked against them.

Uncle Hal refusing to give up on or give in to me after the Andover debacle taught me to do the same for myself. Success wasn't about proving Andover (or Becky Sykes) wrong; it was about proving myself right for believing I was worthy. Now I just needed the right arena to fight the battles that mattered most.

As the summer ended, Evan reached out to me with an intriguing offer, prompting me to adjust course yet again. I valued a legal education, but practicing law was not my calling. I needed to work directly in schools if I wanted to help change the landscape of urban public education. Evan urged me to join him at Uncommon Schools, a new nonprofit created to serve as an umbrella organization to manage charter schools. No matter how challenged, virtually every large high-needs school district—from New York City to Chicago to Los Angeles—can point to pockets of excellence. Uncommon's starting point was that *every* school in a "district" could be excellent. To prove that bold premise, Uncommon was pulling together several leaders of high-performing charters into a collaborative network where we could share experience, ideas, and resources.

When Evan became Uncommon's COO, he asked me to help him launch operations in New York City. I would be superintendent of a New York City network of Uncommon schools modeled on Roxbury Prep (which itself would soon become part of Uncommon's network). Evan wanted me to oversee the hiring and evaluation of staff as well as curriculum development. I would also determine what programs and initiatives we needed to add on as our network grew. My first project would be an elementary school under construction in Bedford-Stuyvesant.

I didn't think twice about accepting Evan's offer, even knowing it would mean striking a careful balance between family, building Uncommon, and finishing both law school and my dissertation. I began in the fall of 2005, right around the time Melissa and I, having both by then celebrated our thirtieth birthdays, decided to have a second baby. Crazy-busy as we were, growing our family made sense while Melissa was working on her doctorate and we still had Melissa's mom on hand to help us out.

Now I would commute between New York City, New Haven, and Boston. I soon knew every conductor on Amtrak and Metro-North, and every snack in the café car. I was adept at turning a tray table into a makeshift desk, and grateful when there were empty seats next to me to expand my workspace.

The tiny commuter apartment in New Haven was eventually swapped out for a Brooklyn two-bedroom I shared with a young cousin who was trying to break into the performance world as a singer and dancer. We rarely saw each other.

We welcomed Mireya Samantha Adwoa King on July 3, 2006, and I worked remotely from Boston that summer, reveling in the bliss of being a father and husband. All the stress in the world can evaporate instantly when you cradle a sleeping newborn in your arms or pause for a tea party with a toddler. Law classes weren't in session, and I only had to make periodic trips to New York City for teacher training or critical team meetings with Uncommon. Life slowed down just enough for me to reflect on my own childhood, remembering how my friends used to daydream out loud about everything they wanted if they won the lottery— mansions to live in with home theaters and swimming pools, trips to Disney World, and luxury cars. I would always keep my biggest wish to myself. All I truly wanted was the life of a normal family. Now, at thirty-one, I was the luckiest man on the earth.

There's no denying those years were challenging with two small children, but they were also deeply fulfilling and fun. Knowing that my own girls would be among millions of kids entering the public school system within a few short years and understanding what a lifelong impact that stood to have on them, my determination to ensure a gold-standard public education for every child grew even fiercer.

That fall, Uncommon prepared to launch the New York City network with a showstopper.

Excellence Boys Charter School had been in the works for a couple of years by the time I was hired and became its superintendent. The first classes were already full, and the waiting lists long. Classes were being held at a temporary facility while Uncommon built Excellence a new home.

The site chosen had originally been the location of P.S. 70, an elementary school built back in 1882 on a residential street in Bedford-Stuyvesant, a historically African-American section of Brooklyn. Abandoned after a major fire in the 1970s, the school had remained a hulking, burned-out eyesore ever since. It was a haven for drug dealers and users, sex workers, cock-fight organizers, and anyone else with dangerous reasons to seek a hideaway. With $30 million in philanthropic donations raised through Robin Hood (a widely respected New York City foundation) and another $6 million personally from Robin Hood founder Paul Tudor Jones, Uncommon bought the property and announced plans to build a state-of-the-art public charter school for local boys.

Robert A. M. Stern, esteemed dean of Yale's School of Architecture, agreed to design the new building. Uncommon gut-renovated the charred remains of P.S. 70, shoveling out empty crack vials and chasing off stray dogs as the construction crews went to work. An elegant, block-long redbrick building rose up from the rubble—90,000 square feet all told. Inside, there was a library with 10,000 books donated by book publishers Scholastic and HarperCollins and reading nooks on every floor. There were music and art studios and a gymnasium with a climbing wall. The rooftop boasted a playing field with artificial turf and views of the skyline.

Uncommon had hired Jabali Sawicki away from Roxbury Prep to be principal, with a commitment to coach him as the talented young teacher assumed his first role as an administrator while the school was still in its temporary quarters. Jabali brought the Spirit Stick with him, along with the Friday tradition of raucous "community meetings." When the school opened the doors of its state-of-the-art new building in September 2006, the staff welcomed 170 boys in kindergarten through third grade, greeting each child by name and shaking hands as the boys crossed the threshold in their uniforms of starched white shirts and ties, with dress pants and shoes.

During the construction I had pulled a familiar book from the shelves of my own library and began thumbing through the worn pages, looking for a bit of lost history. I knew my father passed through Bed-Stuy, where he had grown up, at points during his career and was curious to see if *Negroes of Achievement in Modern America* would offer any insight about the neighborhood's schools back then. I was surprised by the answer I discovered on page 175:

John King was principal of P.S. 70.

In 1945, after passing the examination to become a principal, my father had been assigned to P.S. 70. His goal was similar to mine, I read: "One of his biggest challenges was to see that pupils under his charge had all the advantages of those in the more prosperous sections of the city. His interest was in human relations—and in presenting the correct general principles and methods of teaching, insofar as he was able." As I read about the man I never really knew, I felt, as an educator, a kinship I had never known as a son.

Now it was my turn to take on the very same challenges in the same place, rescued from the ashes and made whole again.

CHAPTER NINE

THE DOOR OF NO RETURN IS A LOW, NARROW ARCHWAY OF
stone, with an iron gate that swings open to the rocky shore on
the Gulf of Guinea, where the kidnappers' ships once waited to
carry away millions of men and women to a life of enslavement.
I stood there with my wife and two young daughters, on my first
trip to Africa, lost in troubling thought.

Elmina Castle, a few hours' drive from the Ghanaian capital
of Accra, is now a UNESCO World Heritage Site, its history as
a principal depot for the imprisonment, torture, rape, auction-
ing, and branding of enslaved Africans bound for Europe and
the Americas recounted by tour guides and exhibits in a small
museum within the huge hilltop fortress. But that day, history
felt more intimate than the sprawling compound, more immediate. No books I had read, no lessons I had taught, ever had the
impact I felt merely standing in that infamous portal.

I spotted the colorful skiffs bobbing in the surf below us and thought about the similar small boats that used to ferry the newly sold souls from Elmina to the huge trade ships anchored in deeper water nearby. I wondered about any surviving children and elders left behind in their tribal villages in the interior, hiding and terrified. I wondered, too, about the generations born into slavery, children trapped in an oppressive America where education was denied and literacy outlawed for people of color. Education, for them, came from the wisdom of their elders, the stories they told, the examples they set, the knowledge they gleaned from nature, or from what they observed or overheard when serving white people. As a history teacher and scholar, I was familiar with the story of Elmina and the forty or so other "slave castles"—actually large commercial fortresses—that European traders erected along the "Gold Coast" of West Africa in what is now Ghana. Yet I was unprepared for the shock of standing in that doorway.

I had steeped myself in written accounts of the harrowing journey across the Atlantic Middle Passage. I could imagine the physical misery of people chained together with no fresh air or sunshine, with scant food or fresh water, trapped in the fevered heat and stench of people sick or dying from malaria or yellow fever. I could imagine the blood and pus seeping from open wounds left by the heavy chains, the leg irons, the lash. I could imagine the sounds of people weeping and crying out in agony. What was beyond my imagination was the pain of being ripped away from my family, the panic of not knowing where I was going, or if I would ever see them again.

We had begun the group tour in the fortress's main courtyard, where a small Catholic church the Portuguese had built had been converted to a human auction house by the conquering Dutch.

We climbed to the castle's top floor, where the governors, traders, and other elite European guests enjoyed luxurious suites with wooden floors and windows that looked out over the sparkling water and palm trees swaying in the tropical breeze. Beneath them were the dungeons, a warren of dank and narrow stone passages where more than two hundred prisoners would have been jammed at once, waiting for their designated ships, sometimes for months. Amina (way too young to grasp the historical context) was fascinated by the colony of bats her grandfather pointed out in one corner. Without a word, our guide suddenly doused his flashlight, and the room fell pitch black, leaving us all to contemplate this difficult place for a few silent minutes. Melissa and I both felt a shiver down our spines despite the oppressive Sub-Saharan heat, feeling the reality of the impenetrable walls closing in on us as we clutched each other's hands in the utter darkness.

Where Monticello incited my rage, Elmina brought despair. I was humbled by the reminder, though, that sometimes the most powerful teacher is not a person, but a place.

For me, Ghana held more of an immediate family tie than any sense of an ancestral one, since Melissa was born there and most of her maternal relatives still live there. My first impression, leaving the airport, had been to notice how similar the country seemed to Puerto Rico, on the surface. The climate was immediately tropical, and Accra had a similar mix of hyper-modern development butting right up against folks living in shanty houses. I was intrigued by the different types of buildings so close together and learned that there is no traditional zoning; people build where they can, on a plot they can afford. They finance houses in a build-as-you-go manner rather than going deeply into debt. It isn't uncommon to see houses with only a few walls up and maybe a couple of rooms, perched on a much larger foundation so they can add on at their own pace—a real-life geometry equation unfolding before their children's eyes, and frankly far more interesting than constructing triangles or a rhombus with a compass in a classroom. In their retirement, Melissa's parents were splitting their time between the United States and Accra, where Biff was teaching at the university. They had bought a finished house in a more suburban area within the city limits. Adwoa kept busy with family, friends, and projects. Their deep knowledge and love for Ghana and its culture made my first visit intimate and memorable. Besides Elmina, the must-see list for me included the famed Makola open-air market and a trip to the home where W. E. B. Du Bois and his wife, Shirley, lived in his final years.

Du Bois was ninety-three when the couple moved to Ghana at the invitation of President Kwame Nkrumah, who offered them a comfortable seven-room bungalow on an acre of land. It was there that the sociologist, writer, activist, and philosopher continued to work on his *Encyclopedia Africana* project until his death two years later, in 1963.

The life of Du Bois—the first African-American to earn a doctorate at Harvard, one of the founders of the NAACP, and pivotal historian of the Reconstruction who challenged how its story had been misrepresented—always fascinated me. Standing in his study, I remembered his descriptions of his summers teaching in rural Tennessee in his landmark book *The Souls of Black Folk*. Seeing firsthand how racism operated to deny opportunity lit a fire in Du Bois around seeking systemic change. What I had experienced as a teacher had similarly inspired me to seek scale change, but I wondered whether I was pushing hard enough, fast enough. I loved the beacon of promise outside the system that we were building at Uncommon. At the same time, though, I felt a pull to actually get inside the system and try from within to nudge it closer to the notions of equity, opportunity, and civic engagement I thought should animate public education.

The flip side of Ghana's historic sites for deep reflection would have to be the open-air Makola Market—the country's largest— where thousands of vendors and shoppers haggle each day in a good-humored ritual that's as much about theater as it is about bartering, which I saw firsthand when my mother-in-law morphed into an entirely different human being as we slowly made our way through the labyrinth of stalls. Adwoa, normally congenial but proper, her countenance that of the composed physician that she is, suddenly became hyper-animated over the cost of a yard of kente cloth (to be used to make a shirt for Biff) or a necklace for Melissa. "How much?" wasn't so much a question as a thrown gauntlet, an opening parry recognized and respected by both parties involved in the verbal duel about to begin. I'm pretty sure the vendor's response didn't matter at this point, because Adwoa would have responded the same—she was a highly skilled bargainer, it turned out. If the marketplace were a Vegas casino, security probably would have red-flagged her. "What? That's ridiculous!" Adwoa would exclaim, contorting her facial expression into exaggerated dismay. Even her posture, usually ramrod straight, would change and become somehow more fluid, arms sweeping, hands flicking in dismissive gesture before she turned dramatically on her heel as if to huff off. Which both parties knew she wasn't going to actually do. The vendors had their individual styles of response and sequence of feigned emotions, too—hurt, insulted, placating, but in the end, usually reasonable. It reminded me of the code-switching we urged our students back home to master and deploy so they could toggle seamlessly between the rapid-fire banter they bounced off each other on their block to the more formal speaking style they would need for college interviews. It's not about acting; it's about finding your authentic self in shifting environments.

The wares on offer at Makola seemed endless: fresh fruits, vegetables, and proteins I had never seen before, piled high. More familiar staples, like tomatoes, could be stacked one atop the other three or four high, yet still be utterly unblemished, literally picked that morning. The vendors—the majority of them women—called out to us, offering samples, the ones with myriad local chiles for sale bursting into laughter whenever an unwary tourist bit into the hottest ones. There were live land snails the size of softballs. My senses were twitching like live wires—one stall would bring the pungent smell of dried tilapia, pulled from the lake, salted, and spread out to dry in the sun, then a stall nearby would counter with the sweet aroma of fresh doughnuts being deep-fried. There were time warps and culture clashes at every turn: Vintage Ashanti masks sold next to Matchbox cars, or Barbies overlooking the artists sewing beads and sequins onto fabric customers had just purchased from patterned bolts. Customers balancing their purchases and vendors balancing fresh inventory atop their heads—baskets of produce, towers of pots and housewares, even tubs of palm oil—wove through the jostling crowd graceful as ballerinas. Artisans carved and painted wooden masks in makeshift woodshops while drummers in lawn chairs performed outside the stalls where the instruments were being made. Amina and Mireya were wide-eyed and enchanted. I realized that what they were absorbing was more than entertainment—this culture belonged to them, and they would grow up knowing Ghana as a motherland. We left Ghana with a story of our own to tell, a piece of family lore, when Mireya pulled herself to her feet for the first time and attempted, on African soil, her first wobbly steps.

Returning to the States, I bade a fond farewell to both Roxbury Prep and Massachusetts and moved my family back to my homeland—New York City.

We rented the top two floors of a four-story brownstone in Clinton Hill, a diverse neighborhood adjacent to rapidly gentrifying Fort Greene, on a block just around the corner from where Christopher Wallace, aka Notorious B.I.G., was born. Melissa got a great job in a research department at Scholastic, and we enrolled Amina in a diverse Montessori preschool above a Park Slope church, and Mireya in a one-room daycare in Cobble Hill. Being back in Brooklyn felt like a homecoming.

Playgrounds were at the top of our list of places to discover, and Amina quickly identified her favorites to visit. We zeroed in on kid-friendly restaurants, and bounced a lot between Two Boots, which gave kids pizza dough to play with, and Bogota, a Colombian bistro that handed out colorful bendy Wikki Stix with the children's menu. Wikki Stix were like pipe cleaners—only made of sticky wax-covered yarn, so no warnings necessary about not putting out an eye—and you could shape them into different figures. Mireya and Amina loved to craft elaborate scenes of animals, houses, and people sprawling across the wooden table.

After the kids were asleep, I would sneak out to spend weeknights studying at a popular Park Slope café called the Tea

Lounge. The Tea Lounge was a bring-it-on slap in the face to the ever-expanding Starbucks chain. Inside, long wooden community tables nudged up against mismatched "vintage" sofas and armchairs with their own coffee tables. The scattershot furniture arrangement all but mandated mingling, whether intentional or unavoidable, as if the design team consisted of a sly matchmaker and a utopian communard. Rattan ceiling fans summoned Casablanca overhead, and a blue awning paid homage to Paris outside. The extensive chalkboard menu offered organic coffees as well as tea, plus a creative array of cocktails, sandwiches, soups, salads, and appetizers. Anything from a mango lassi to a tequila gimlet. I could snack on a simple grilled cheese or a hot turkey Reuben while cranking out my dissertation. There was live music some evenings, and interesting chatter no matter what the hour. On Saturdays I would really hunker down, working within a sea of yuppie moms with designer strollers, feeding their toddlers oatmeal and fresh berries as they compared notes on getting into elite nursery schools and hyper-competitive pre-Ks with application packets that looked fatter than the ones I'd filled out for Harvard. Afternoons segued to the work-from-home types with their laptops; attractive women tended to wear headphones. My favorite was the night shift, when couples on dates moved in. The Tea Lounge was the kind of place you could use to drag a good first date out longer or put an early end to a bad second one. ("I'll just have an avocado toast.") I kept an ear cocked for the awkward small talk of first encounters, which was always fun. The crowd was reliably eclectic, a mix that could just as easily be corporate lawyers and punk rockers with a dash of aspiring actors as Wall Street analysts, tourists, and failed playwrights. Late one night, I found myself sitting not too far from Representative

Anthony Weiner and a lovely woman who would likely wish someday that she had worn headphones. (The Democratic congressman was still several years away from jail time over a sexting scandal that included sending lewd photos to a minor.) Minding your own business took a lot of self-discipline (plus earphones) at the Tea Lounge.

Maybe it was that feeling of settling in back "home" that prompted me to try to reconnect with Gil. Whenever I had tried to reach out to my brother over the years, I would convince myself that he was doing better and getting his life together. During our calls, he sounded convincing. How much he was drinking (or not) was never clear until I actually saw him.

Melissa wanted me to be cautious. Her experience of Gil encounters was that I always somehow emerged wounded. She wasn't wrong.

One memorable trip I had made to see Gil in Florida early in our marriage served as Melissa's metaphor for our brotherhood: It was an incredibly hot afternoon in Jacksonville, and Gil and I were going to see a Jaguars game. He had brought a football and wanted me to play catch with him in the parking lot. He was like a kid, egging me on. "Run long, I'll pass," he commanded. I ran out, and he purposely threw the ball far in front of me, laughing. I didn't want to fail; I was a kid again. So I kept running full-on, totally focused on the ball, in this suddenly intense competition. I tripped on a parking space curb and went flying, hitting the asphalt with a smack, then skidding. The pain was instant and excruciating. I had skinned every bit of flesh off one knee, twisted my ankle, and broken a toe.

I couldn't admit to Gil that I was hurt. I popped up from the ground to go into the game, sat, and watched it while baking in the 95-degree sun with no shade, miserable every moment. Gil was oblivious and, of course, drinking. I went to the bathroom and wrapped my bloody knee with toilet paper.

Try hard, fall hard, deny pain, seethe with anger, hide wounds. That was my ritual with my brother.

Amina was going on five and Mireya just two years old when I saw Gil for the last time. He was about forty-five by then, his dark hair now salt-and-pepper. Charming, likable, super smart as always, but never really able to get a toehold on life. I didn't know whether the laissez-faire attitude was cause or effect. The girls were excited to meet their uncle when he came to visit and stay with us for a few days. He was great with the kids, silly and playful; there were good moments that weekend. Gil was always nervous around Melissa, sensing her reservations about him. Their relationship was confined to smiles and cordial small talk. Gil brought a bottle of vodka with him, which we pretended not to notice, and he drank steadily, and mostly stealthily, throughout his stay. I was disappointed, but didn't want to pick a fight.

On his second day, we went to visit a cousin from the Bronx who had recently married a wealthy Manhattan businessman. They lived in a posh high-rise on the Upper West Side, more than twenty floors up on the elevator. The Hudson River view from their living room was beautiful as we enjoyed drinks and hors d'oeuvres. Gil had gotten a head start on the cocktail hour before we even left our house and kept drinking steadily. He was toasted when he walked out onto the balcony. I went with him, Amina trailing behind me. Gil walked toward the balcony's waist-high glass retainer wall, and Amina scampered up to him. He picked her up and held her with one arm while using the other to point out New Jersey on the other side of the river. I immediately tensed. An incredible panic gripped me, a feeling sick and familiar, as he took a few steps closer to the edge, pointing out other sights. I froze, unable to speak or move. He kept talking and pointing and stepping closer and closer to the barrier, until he was right there, holding my daughter in one arm with her small body high above the wall's railing. A familiar survival instinct commanded me to remain perfectly still. I knew if I said something—if I shouted at Gil or lunged to grab Amina—it would make things worse. Gil went through life courting disaster and was in his element now. If he registered my fear, he would heighten the danger to mock or bully me with his own disdain, just to feel in control. All of this was happening in a matter of seconds that felt like years. Then he put Amina down—safe, smiling, and oblivious—and we all went inside.

I fumed in silence. I hated how helpless I felt seeing my child, so innocent and vulnerable, imperiled by my brother, so reckless and unpredictable. As a child, I had felt it was my duty to stay by Gil's side as he sped raging drunk down the Long Island Expressway. I owed him. As a father that day, I realized that I could no longer feel a need to repay him. I couldn't see any path to protecting my children in Gil's presence—not when intervention would risk egging him on. I couldn't ever put my girls in that situation again.

I just had to get through the next day. Once he left, I was done with my brother.

"I can't do this until you get help," I said the next time he called. He didn't call back after that. I finally understood that sometimes making peace means walking away, and the sadness of that is at least less sad than if I had stayed.

I ended up spending nearly four years as managing director of Uncommon Schools, gratified by the results we saw: multiple new schools achieving the same sort of excellent academic results as the original schools that had inspired Uncommon's founding, like Roxbury Prep.

Still, the question was ever-present in my mind: Can we do more for the kids? Would it work on a much larger scale?

I wanted to keep leveling up the bar. When the state's new education commissioner, David Steiner, called to ask me to be his senior deputy, I wondered if this might be my chance. David had been the dean of the School of Education at Hunter College (my mother's alma mater) and had spent his career in higher education institutions. He wanted a deputy with a K–12 background who could bring a focus on high-needs students. He made a very persuasive pitch about all we could accomplish together, particularly in partnership with the Obama administration.

When I broached the idea with Melissa, she was skeptical. Leaving Brooklyn—including our friends and all the things we loved about New York City—was not at all appealing. However, I had an ace up my sleeve: Zillow.

We had begun looking for a house in Brooklyn, and with our limited budget, the search largely consisted of evaluating what we were willing to give up. Could we get used to a refrigerator in the dining room? A third bedroom that was really a converted walk-in closet? Linoleum in every room? However, in the Albany area, we could get twice as much house for half as much money. I sold Melissa on wonderful, modern suburban homes with three bedrooms for our family, a spare bedroom for her parents, a study, a huge yard, a two-car garage, and more. A trip around the Albany suburbs with a Realtor sealed the deal. Melissa negotiated a hybrid arrangement with Scholastic and would commute from Albany back to New York City one day a week. With a trusted babysitter to fill in the after-school gaps, at least one parent would still always be home for dinner and to tuck the girls in. We had a solid plan, and we were pros by now when it came to packing up and settling into a new place.

Surprisingly, this go-around was different. Neither one of us predicted the culture shock coming. And for me professionally, Albany would deliver an even tougher challenge.

CHAPTER TEN

THE FIRST THING I NOTICED WAS THE UNSPOKEN TITLE THAT trailed me around the sleepy capital from the start, a mantle I thought I had discarded in Puerto Rico. Once again, I was the Only Black Guy (and the Only Latino Guy, for that matter). Whether I was in meetings at the State Education Department or went out to eat a fancy lunch or dinner in Albany, I usually integrated the room (or was one of a very small number of people of color). The neighborhoods often seemed to be almost exclusively Black or white, literally, with people of color concentrated in the city and present only in much smaller numbers in the suburbs.

Amina wondered where the people with interesting tattoos and dyed blue hair were. Melissa and I missed lengthy debates over what kind of ethnic food to try on a date night.

Too often the Albany area gave the impression that economic and racial inclusion were big problems but not of pressing concern. As an educator and data cruncher, I could readily see evidence of that in the opportunity and achievement gaps between kids of color attending public schools in lower-income urban neighborhoods and kids attending public schools in predominantly white suburbs.

My first challenge in the new job was to lay the groundwork for New York's adoption of the Common Core standards for teaching and learning in English and math, which had been developed jointly by a coalition of states. The goal was to ensure all high school graduates—no matter their zip code or family income—were prepared for success in college and careers. The Common Core's standards were grounded in evidence about what it would take to close equity gaps. The promise was that a shift in what teachers emphasized would help hone critical thinking and problem solving to better prepare students for the demands of college. The Common Core also envisioned more work to build vocabulary, writing skills, and background knowledge, along with more problem solving and application in math rather than just rote memorization of formulas.

My primary focus as deputy commissioner was to prepare New York State's grant application for funds from the US Department of Education's $4 billion Race to the Top competition. This would give us the resources to help make Common Core implementation successful. Created by President Obama to inspire and reward education improvements in K–12 schools, Race to the Top judged states vying for prize money based on a 500-point measure of specific criteria.

States' applications were scored based on adopting and implementing college and career readiness standards, allowing the number of charter schools to increase, turning around the lowest-performing schools, strengthening data systems to provide teachers and parents with better information about students' progress, and evaluating teachers and principals based on performance. The latter would prove the most contentious, as I would discover soon enough.

David and I didn't have time to chart the political waters. We set sail when the winds and current suited us and dove right into working with the Board of Regents (New York's state board of education appointed by the legislature) to develop the crucial application.

We lost in the first round of awards—only two states were selected by the US Education Department to receive Race to the Top funding, Delaware and Tennessee—largely because New York had not yet caught up with all of the bold reforms the Obama administration was championing. As Albany newcomers, neither of us had developed the relationships yet to negotiate with all the stakeholders whose buy-in was essential, such as teachers unions, or to persuade the legislature to implement the kind of policies Race to the Top demanded. In the next round with the feds, David and I had to make sure New York didn't end up empty-handed.

Ironically, the equal-education quest I had long grappled with professionally posed a personal dilemma now that I was a parent. Like most parents, Melissa and I put good schools at the top of our priority list when we began house hunting around the Albany area. Bustling cities were our natural habitat; we knew we weren't going to be able to replicate the diverse, urban lifestyle that made us love Brooklyn, but we held out hope for a neighborhood with its own charms. As long as our kids were happy, we'd be fine. We did our research and eventually zeroed in on a safe, semi-rural suburb whose public schools were high-performing and widely respected. We bought our first house based on that. It was basically the same template Gil had used twenty years earlier when he and I moved to Smithtown, Long Island.

Amina would be enrolling in an elementary school in a vaunted district. She was excited about eating lunch in a cafeteria and making new friends. We were surprised and disheartened to see her J-factor quickly flag.

"Mommy, first graders here are all younger than first graders in Brooklyn," she reported early on. Melissa was puzzled. Why did Amina think that? "Because first graders here can't read yet," Amina elaborated.

Amina had picked up reading at three. Amina wasn't complaining or acting out in her new class, so we let it go. As teachers, Melissa and I recognized that Amina's teacher was "teaching to the middle," a frequent practice—particularly for a busy teacher who probably wished she had the time to differentiate more. We happen to have a family rule that everyone must always be reading something for pleasure; Amina loved books, and her literacy wasn't going to suffer.

Amina may have not felt challenged by her new school, but Melissa and I did.

Amina was one of only a few Black or brown kids in the entire elementary school, and the only one in her class. She was a city kid in a school where some peers lived on farms their families had owned for generations. Normally highly social and extroverted, she didn't share much with us about her new classmates, and none of the neighborhood kids knocked on our door asking to play. Several months into the school year, Melissa and I realized Amina had not been invited to a single birthday party. Melissa and I weren't invited to any get-togethers, either. I guiltily wondered whether our neighbors were steering a wide berth because I was the deputy commissioner and my position somehow made socializing awkward.

In January, Amina's isolation became moot when she came home with exciting news. A new kid named Felix had just moved to town from California. Felix was really nice, and everybody liked him. He sat next to Amina and they instantly became friends. Each weekday brought fresh news about Felix.

Felix was smart. He was cute. Felix was popular with girls but liked Amina best. Felix and Amina ate lunch together and played every recess. Melissa was eager to meet Felix and his mom at the next school event to invite them over for a playdate. She was disappointed that Felix was out sick that day, but Amina seemed unfazed, content with the school hours she got to spend with her new pal. At the end of the school year, she brought home a little hand-crafted yearbook her teacher had put together for everyone, with a page for each child featuring a drawing they had made. Melissa flipped through the pages, her anxiety building like a scene from "The Shining," until it finally hit her on the last page:

"Oh my God, she made him up!" she exclaimed. "Amina, there is no Felix, is there? Felix is not real!"

The truth was more upsetting than the lie. Amina was quite bored and lonely and just invented the perfect solution. Felix made her Albany life more interesting than any of us had. Amina sheepishly admitted that there was no Felix, but clearly didn't want to discuss it.

Mireya, on the other hand, was more than vocal about her educational environment, and began throwing daily tantrums about her preschool. She declared she wasn't going with the kind of fierce conviction usually reserved for college sit-ins.

We decided to check out the pre-K at a local Montessori elementary school for her instead. When we arrived for our scheduled visit, it was Amina who walked in, looked around at the familiar classroom materials, and immediately asked, "Can I go here? When can I go here?"

We ended up enrolling both girls. Felix vanished as quickly as he had appeared. Amina made lots of new friends, and Mireya was eager to go to preschool again. Melissa got her city-and-friends fix the days she worked at the Scholastic offices in Manhattan.

When the second round of Race to the Top grants were awarded, New York scored second highest among the ten winners. Massachusetts scored higher by a hair. Thanks to our progress in securing broad stakeholder buy-in and new legislation (including raising a cap on the number of charter schools allowed in the state and a new teacher-evaluation system), we were awarded $700 million.

With the federal windfall, we had the means to ramp up the transition to Common Core standards by providing more resources and training for the thousands of educators at ground level who would have to implement the policy. To his credit, as commissioner, David Steiner had been an early champion of helping teachers by providing high-quality instructional materials. I knew from my experience as a teacher and a principal that just telling teachers to teach to higher standards wouldn't be enough. We needed to provide the tools. Otherwise, what we would be asking of them was tantamount to architects handing over blueprints to skilled carpenters and expecting them to erect the country's first skyscraper with hammers and nails, without providing any engineers, cranes, or special training.

I was charged with figuring out how to deliver on our vision. We decided to build an on-line platform called EngageNY.org for sharing with New York state teachers free exceptional Common Core curricula for English Language Arts and Math developed via our Race to the Top funding.

We selected the best partners through a competitive process, and they then mobilized armies of fantastic teachers and curriculum writers to develop new materials, including Core Knowledge for PreK–2 English Language Arts, an organization that had grown out of research on the importance of building background knowledge and students' vocabulary alongside systematic phonics instruction; Expeditionary Learning for 3–8 English Language Arts, a network of schools that evolved from Outward Bound programs and that focused on project-based learning infused with community building; and Eureka Math, an innovative math curriculum focused on problem solving and deeper conceptual understanding.

We knew we had to pair the new curricula with intensive professional development and set up support teams in every region of the state and then began bringing them to Albany every other month for train-the-trainer sessions we called Network Team Institutes.

Imagine hundreds of enthusiastic teachers and teacher-leaders in an Albany hotel ballroom communing over the best probing questions to ask students about Chapter 2 of *Esperanza Rising* by Pam Muñoz Ryan, or the keys to unlocking student understanding of proportional reasoning.

I spent the first year and a half sorting out the nuts and bolts to essentially build this massive ship to help teachers make their way toward better instructional practice. It was exhilarating and inspiring. The policy was in place; the particulars of what we would need to change in classrooms and how to do so were identified. We seemed to be all geared up.

Then the commissioner abruptly decided to leave. While David was proud of what we were building, he didn't love the day-to-day politics and he missed "the life of the academy"—the world of writing, research, and teaching on a campus—so he returned to Hunter. The Board of Regents asked me to succeed him. I became the first African-American and first Latino to hold the job and, at thirty-six, one of the youngest state education leaders in the country.

My promotion came with a daunting job description. I would be overseeing some 3.1 million students; more than 7,000 public and independent elementary and secondary schools (for which we were responsible for standards, assessments, data, state funding, civil rights enforcement, and more); 270 public, independent, and proprietary colleges and universities (for which we were a regulator); 7,000 libraries; 900 museums; 25 public broadcasting facilities; 3,000 historical repositories; 436 proprietary schools; 52 professions encompassing more than 850,000 licensees plus 240,000 certified educators; and services for children and adults with disabilities. It also came with the opportunity to meet countless New Yorkers who were dedicating their lives to creating the best education imaginable to prepare today's children for tomorrow's challenges, from teachers in small rural schoolhouses to professors in world-class universities.

When I wasn't in Albany, I was crisscrossing the state visiting school districts, college campuses, museums, and all manner of educational institutions to see what was happening on the ground.

What I saw in classrooms implementing the new curricula inspired me. In schools where a year earlier I had seen teachers drilling fifth grade students on strategies for answering multiple-choice questions about dry passages in a textbook, I now saw teachers and students guided by the Common Core using nonfiction and text-based discussions and the Expeditionary Learning curriculum to talk about the implications of Article I of the UN's Universal Declaration of Human Rights, which states, "All human beings are born free and equal in dignity and rights. They are endowed with reason and conscience and should act towards one another in a spirit of brotherhood." Rather than students memorizing tricks for dividing mixed numbers, students were essentially crafting the problem using shapes and blocks, just as Amina and Mireya would in their Montessori classrooms, so they could see the difference between 5½ divided by 2 as opposed to 5½ divided by a ½.

Best of all were the conversations with principals and teachers telling me about how engaged their students were and how much rapid progress they were seeing.

Melissa was sometimes taken aback by the level of enthusiasm for the curricular materials and the professional development on EngageNY that we encountered in our day-to-day lives. Once we went for a date night to Saratoga Springs, where the draw of the racetrack has translated into fancy stores, multiple upscale restaurants, and some cool music places in a cute downtown shopping area. We found a bar where a DJ was playing on a large outdoor patio, and as we started to dance, we could see a group of around ten women standing on the other side of the patio eyeing us. After a few minutes, one of them came over and explained that they were teachers attending a weekend professional development session on the EngageNY curricular materials. They had seen me talking about the Common Core instructional shifts in a video and told me how happy it made them to see a high-level education administrator so passionate about the classroom and engaged with the nuances of teaching and learning. Within seconds, Melissa had been handed multiple phones to take photos of the teachers posing with me. We enjoyed a deep conversation about how quickly their first graders' vocabularies were growing, thanks to the Core Knowledge units on early world civilizations and animals and habitats.

As the conversation ended, they thanked me for EngageNY, saying this was the first district-sponsored workshop they could remember that had made a real difference for their students' learning.

Visiting schools was always a joy. I particularly made sure to spend time in our highest-needs districts, visiting both turn-around schools and new schools trying to close gaps in academic achievement and provide students with paths to upward mobility.

I was starstruck when I first met President Obama, joining him for a visit to a turnaround high school in Brooklyn. His 2008 campaign had so inspired me, his inaugural address had so moved me, and his Race to the Top had defined my time in the commissioner's office. I wished I could have more of his time, but in our brief conversation, I did at least manage to express my gratitude for his intense focus on improving educational outcomes for the students most often left behind.

Uncle Hal passed that summer, at the age of ninety-one. His loss was devastating, but the lessons he taught me about integrity and perseverance burned brighter than ever. As a Tuskegee Airman, his service long unacknowledged, his courage dismissed, he could have easily given in to bitterness and defeat. Instead, he lived a life of purpose, never letting *For what?* replace the *Why?* in his many challenges and endeavors. He and my Aunt Jean were interred at Arlington National Cemetery, a powerful reflection of their shared patriotism and devotion to service.

By fall of 2013, two things were clear: (1) EngageNY.org was a runaway hit with districts, schools, and teachers throughout the state and across the country, with users raving about how rigorous and engaging the rapidly growing body of high-quality instructional materials was; and (2) storm clouds were gathering.

Although the Common Core had been developed by states, not the federal government, and the federal government was actually prohibited from dictating curricula in schools, Race to the Top had deeply entangled the Common Core with the Obama administration in the minds of many on the right, so much so that it began to be called "Obamacore" in some places.

Over time, conservatives (many of whom had publicly supported the Common Core during its creation) began to attack the standards as an example of federal overreach. In the dark corners of social media, Common Core got conflated with all manner of far-right conspiracy theories. One excellent example was the unhinged reaction to *The Librarian of Basra: A True Story from Iraq.* Inspired by a *New York Times* article, the beautifully written and illustrated children's book by Jeanette Winter was featured within the Expeditionary Learning curriculum. The book tells the story of a librarian in war-torn Iraq whose city library was being used by the Iraqi military as a command post. Fearing the library might be bombed, the librarian smuggled thousands of library books into her home in order to preserve them. It is a lovely story about the power and beauty of books, but in the hands of conspiracy mongers, it became something else entirely.

Emails and online posts claimed the Common Core was a vehicle for anti-American propaganda (since the potential bombs could have been American, though the book itself did not say so) or even more frightening, a tool to "achieve President Obama's goal of converting children into Muslims."

Even more worrisome, the Common Core was being conflated by some parents and educators with the teacher evaluation requirements of Race to the Top and federal testing required by the 2002 No Child Left Behind Act. The latter had passed with strong bipartisan support, championed by then-President George W. Bush and Senator Ted Kennedy, but enthusiasm for the federal law had substantially faded. In conversations with teachers and parents as I visited schools, I would also sometimes hear Common Core blamed for shorter science and social studies periods in elementary schools. That, too, could be traced back to No Child Left Behind, which emphasized school accountability for reading and math scores.

It was incredibly frustrating to encounter so much confusion. We had some serious communication gaps to fill, not just in New York but nationally. Try as I might to separate the issues, the Common Core was increasingly becoming a grab bag for complaints about all of K–12's shortcomings.

Teacher evaluation was a particular lightning rod. Even though New York's evaluation law was passed as part of the Race to the Top legislative package with the support of the state's teachers union, there was always palpable discomfort among many teachers with the inclusion of students' progress (or lack thereof) on state tests in individual teacher evaluations even at a modest level. Then-Governor Andrew Cuomo didn't help matters, arguing that the state's evaluation law wasn't "tough enough" and regularly referring to the evaluation system as a tool for "getting rid of bad teachers" rather than a tool for continuous improvement, which was my hope.

With the skies darkening, I began to work with the New York State PTA on putting together a series of five town hall forums to address concerns and answer questions about Common Core's tougher expectations. With naive calm and confidence—and not much experience being in the public eye to the degree I now was as commissioner—I walked straight into the tempest.

The auditorium was packed and buzzing at my first stop, a suburban high school in Spackenkill, just outside of Poughkeepsie. I took the stage and began to speak, trying to ignore the boos and the shouts of hecklers. Some of the parents were outraged over the low scores from the first round of tests, and worried how much classroom time would now be used for test prep. Some teachers and union representatives were upset over the teacher evaluation law and job security being tied in any way to their students' scores. Parents and teachers who had come to learn more seemed as taken aback as I was by the tone. As I tried to correct some of the misinformation circulating about our implementation of Common Core and what it would mean, the heckling just became more intense. The jeers turned nastier and I could feel the menace crest like a wave. One parent called me out for sending my own daughters to Montessori instead of public school. I tamped down my anger about my family being dragged into the debate and pointed out that their Montessori school was already hewing to the very same instructional approaches called for in the Common Core standards. The "forum" by then was providing way more heat than light. So much so that security had to escort me out of the building when it ended. I was both shocked and saddened but held fast to my conviction that the work I saw in the classrooms I visited weekly across the state was the right work and had tremendous potential to help students.

I temporarily suspended the forums until my staff and I could reassess and recalibrate. Both online and in person, though, the vitriol toward me kept building. A busload of sign-toting protesters was dropped off in front of our building, demanding my resignation. Colleagues reported hearing me called a Bolshevik, a communist, and—though never to my face—racial slurs.

I decided to resume the town halls and schedule more than three times as many in different parts of the state. This time, though, I would be part of a panel, if only to remind everyone that the Race to the Top application and the package of policies and laws it represented had been the joint work of the Board of Regents, the governor and legislature, and a broad coalition of stakeholders including the statewide teachers union, the school boards association, the superintendents, and the PTA.

I brushed off a colleague's urging to wear a bulletproof vest in public but felt a bolt of fear when a troll sent a message to the effect of "our kids aren't safe, so neither are yours" and named Amina and Mireya's school.

Throughout, my Board Chair Merryl Tisch was a stalwart champion of higher standards and a wise counselor. Amid all the attacks on the Common Core, she never wavered, and she rallied the Board of Regents to defend the standards. She counseled me to be patient and to recognize that meaningful change was always hard. She also insisted that we not let the politics of the Common Core overtake our other priorities, like turning around the lowest-performing schools. She kept urging me to find ways to help the public better understand the progress happening in classrooms.

As an example, she described how a group of parent activists had recently come to see her to slow down a key element of the turnaround work: They wanted her to join them in fighting against a proposal from then–New York City Mayor Bloomberg to close a large failing high school and replace it with three new small schools designed by teams of entrepreneurial educators. Merryl promised to consider the parents' request if they agreed to visit another school. She got a van and brought them to the original P-Tech school (the very school I had visited with President Obama), the first of a network we later expanded across New York State.

At P-Tech, students were admitted by lottery irrespective of prior academic performance and provided with an intensive educational program including college-level courses in a supportive environment. They graduated with a high school diploma, an associate's degree from CUNY, and first in line for a job at IBM. The student body consisted almost entirely of students of color, mostly male, and the school was a "replacement school," meaning a new small school in a building that had previously housed a large failing high school. After the visit, the parent activists changed their minds.

Indeed, the new charters and turnaround schools, especially the small schools in New York City that replaced failing schools and the P-Tech network that we quickly grew to include more than a dozen schools with different employer partners throughout the state, were one of the most important legacies of New York's Race to the Top effort alongside EngageNY.org and the nation-leading new curricula like Core Knowledge, Expeditionary Learning, and Eureka Math.

Not every charter or new, small school succeeded, but many did. Merryl's steadfastness helped us get to the other side of the forums not by just barreling forward, but by engaging with the critics and looking for ways to address legitimate concerns. She reminded me and our team that it is dangerous to simply dismiss everything your opponents have to say, even if you know some of what they are saying isn't true, because you might miss the kernels of truth that can help you be better.

Once the climate had cooled enough for me to reflect instead of react, I publicly conceded that we could have done better preparing everyone for the changes. We could have done a lot more to communicate early what the Common Core would require in terms of instructional change and what it would mean for assessments. We could have given schools and teachers more time to adjust to the changes in a low-stakes context before moving the changes to teacher evaluation forward. We could have taken some of the steps we eventually implemented—like banning P–2 state tests, capping the time spent on state testing, and funding districts to review their testing practices to get rid of redundant, unnecessary, or low-quality locally determined tests—earlier.

Privately, I kicked myself for getting too consumed with the technocratic details and not tuning in enough to the very real, very human anxieties experienced by parents and teachers, and by extension, students. I needed to remind myself more often that having all the facts doesn't necessarily mean you have all the answers.

The strength I found to weather the Common Core storm came in part from the perspective my family brought (including coaching Amina's softball team, which provided the two of us with wonderful bonding time and satisfied my long-deferred childhood dream to be a Little Leaguer) and from a lesson ingrained in me since childhood from my Uncle Dolly, a man I idolized but never knew. Of all the stories my father and Uncle Hal used to tell when they held court, the one that family lore clearly held in highest regard was the legend of their lost brother, the All-American athlete William "Dolly" King. He was eight years younger than my father, the middle son and shining star of their large family. While my father's relatively short physical stature had limited his fervor for sports to serving as manager for football, baseball, and basketball teams in high school, the six-foot-three Dolly's incredible athleticism demanded attention from the first touchdown, home run, or jump shot. He captained all three teams during his high school career.

He went on to play varsity basketball and football at Long Island University, becoming the greatest all-around athlete in the school's history. My father would beam with the kind of pride I hungered to earn when he recounted how Dolly played a winning football game at Ebbets Field, followed by a student-alumni basketball game at LIU, before leading LIU in the National Invitation Tournament at Madison Square Garden—all on Thanksgiving Day, 1939.

What the sportswriters didn't report were the racial slurs by white opponents, who would sometimes purposely bump or even hit Dolly on the court, doing anything they could to throw him off his game. The referees wouldn't intervene on behalf of a "Negro." Professional basketball had yet to integrate. If my father saw Dolly falter, he would seek him out at halftime. "You're buying into what they want you to do. Be bigger than that, do not play into it."

The only thing that kept Uncle Dolly from being drafted by the NBA was his skin color.

He opted to leave LIU a year early to create his own pro team, the Long Island Blackbirds, but was quickly recruited by another heralded team. Within a matter of weeks, Uncle Dolly was playing for the New York Rens, a barnstorming team that won the 1939 World Championship of Professional Basketball beating all-Black and all-white teams from across the country. The Rens were part of the Black Fives—basketball's equivalent of the "Negro Leagues" in baseball—the celebrated teams for African-Americans that boasted dozens of superstars on the court from the turn of the century until professional basketball began lifting its whites-only rule in the late 1940s.

At the age of thirty, Dolly became the first Black player signed by the Rochester Royals, a National Basketball League team that would eventually become the Sacramento Kings in the NBA. By that time, Uncle Dolly was past his prime as a player.

But he was just warming up as an activist and civic leader.

Dolly left the Royals to become a recreational director for a Harlem housing project, and returned to LIU to finish his BA and earn his master's. He became the first Black basketball referee in the Eastern College Athletic Conference and became a prominent professional baseball umpire, as well. In 1964, Dolly was hired as head basketball coach at Borough of Manhattan Community College. My father could still be found in the stands, cheering him on. Dolly remained close to his old teams, too; he was known to play weekend games on occasion with the Rens, and other players looked up to him as a mentor. His son, my cousin Michael, cherishes the story a stranger once told him about Dolly consoling a pro basketball player depressed over an injury that had just ended his career.

Never think of basketball as defining your life, Dolly counseled. *Use basketball to get the next gift that life has to offer.*

Dolly was on a road trip with his team to Binghamton, New York, when chest pains sent him to the local hospital. His worried team gathered at his bedside. "Go and play and win," he reportedly urged them. An hour before the game, Dolly died at the age of fifty-two. His players took the court wearing black armbands.

They played, and they prevailed.

Gone before I was even born, Uncle Dolly was an idea to me rather than a person. What he stood for and who he was were one. He served as a model of excellence, a trailblazer who proved that obstacles can be overcome. I thought of him during that tough, tumultuous period in Albany. He gave purpose to his passion through hard work and discipline. He triumphed over systemic racism.

Early in 2013, after the Brooklyn Nets moved to their beautiful new home at the Barclays Center, I was invited to a special ceremony commemorating the Black Fives Era. The highlight of the evening was the unveiling of a permanent art installation titled "Black Fives at the Barclays Center" in the arena concourse. Six vintage photographs were revealed, creating a floor-to-ceiling mural and there he was, Uncle Dolly, frozen in time, palming a basketball. Triumphant, his heart forever strong.

CHAPTER ELEVEN

Serving in the administration of President Barack Obama as the tenth United States Secretary of Education was the honor of a lifetime.

I had first gotten to know my predecessor, Arne Duncan, through Race to the Top, which he had developed and launched shortly after joining President Barack Obama's first cabinet as education secretary in 2009. In fact, our first conversation was during the early days of the administration, when I was invited to join a planning session based on my work at Roxbury Prep and Uncommon. It was quickly apparent that he shared my passion for public education and a similar vision for how to keep building a stronger system for each and every child who passed through it. When Arne called me in late 2014 to ask if I would consider becoming his deputy, I hesitated. "I will, but only on condition you stay through the end of the term," I told him, worried about whether he would stick around to keep the momentum going behind our shared priorities.

Partnering with Arne to move as many of Obama's major education reforms as far forward as we could with the clock ticking would be the chance of a lifetime. If Arne were to leave before the 2016 election, there was no telling who would replace him. Deputies don't automatically or even traditionally move up to fill an empty cabinet seat. It mattered who I was going to work for if our family was going to give up the life we had painstakingly built in Albany. Professionally, as commissioner, I was beginning to see early academic gains in schools and districts from their transition to the Common Core. Innovative new schools were creating unprecedented opportunities for historically underserved students, and progress was being made to expand dual-language education and foster socioeconomic integration in schools. Moving our family and leaving my team at the New York State Education Department would be hard. Arne promised to stay until Obama's second term ended in January 2017 and assured me that our work in Washington DC would offer opportunities for broader impact.

Melissa and the girls were ecstatic that I could be working in the Obama White House (though technically the Lyndon Baines Johnson Department of Education Building was a short distance away on Maryland Avenue), but the swell of pride was quickly replaced by tears when reality set in. My daughters demanded to know if this meant we would be apart all the time or they would have to move to DC. I guiltily acknowledged that yes, I was counting on my family coming with me. Still, I would have to endure the loneliness of the long-distance commuter until the end of the school year. It was hard on all of us.

I would fly from Albany to DC on Sunday nights, then spend the week working every waking hour, coming "home" to a tiny studio apartment in Silver Spring, Maryland, with an air mattress, a chair, and a TV for watching ESPN until I drifted off to sleep. Then I'd fly back to Albany on Friday nights. Those precious weekends were full of softball for Amina, soccer for Mireya, and preparations for the big move at the end of the school year.

A few months into my tenure as deputy, Arne came into my office, which was next to his in the secretary's suite, and asked to talk. His tone was uncharacteristically somber. For family reasons, he needed to return to his beloved hometown of Chicago. He explained that he wasn't sure what the White House would want to do, but that he was certain I was the best person to succeed him. He would make that clear to the president. I was both completely surprised and deeply humbled. The conversations over the ensuing weeks culminated in President Obama deciding to name me as the next secretary.

On October 2, 2015, Melissa and the girls came with me to the Oval Office to chat with the president before heading to the press conference where my promotion would be announced. As a "civics nerd," I had watched countless presidential announcements of new appointments on C-SPAN, from cabinet members to Supreme Court justices, but I was not prepared for the weight I would feel standing at the podium beside the president.

Arne would be sorely missed, but I had discovered already in my time as his deputy that the biggest source of energy in a presidential administration comes from the people you serve. They are the ones who strengthen your conviction and fire your imagination. Those I encountered—whether people in prison or college presidents, cafeteria workers or Nobel laureates—deepened my fervor for education and equity as they shared their stories, their hopes feeding mine. They were all my teachers. I spent my time as secretary seeking out and listening to as many as I could.

We spend our lives learning, and every lesson shapes us in some way. Part of our hunger for knowledge is to find our place in this world, to understand who we are, and who we might become. There are teachers who touch our lives with intention, like Mr. Osterweil or my Uncle Hal, and those who are unexpected, like Louis Hutt, the charismatic CPA who made me appreciate the power of authenticity. They can be ordinary people we encounter on our journey for a fleeting moment, or extraordinary ones who stay with us for a lifetime. One of them was there to bear witness when I became the tenth US Secretary of Education.

I took over from Arne on January 1 but I was officially confirmed by the US Senate on March 14, and formally sworn in on April 16. Then–Vice President Joe Biden administered the oath of office in a century-old room that once served as the Navy's library, in the Eisenhower Executive Office Building, as those who mattered most to me looked on. My family, close friends, and colleagues from across the years and miles were there to witness it.

In a fortuitous twist of fate, my time as commissioner of education for New York State had led me to reconnect with Mr. Osterweil. His partner, Ross, an elementary school principal on Long Island, participated in the Network Team Institutes on the Common Core. As a result, I was able not only to see Mr. Osterweil again for the first time in years, but to have Amina and Mireya spend time with him—including a fabulous visit together to the Metropolitan Museum of Art, which brought back so many wonderful memories of our class field trips. To my great joy, I was able to invite him to attend my swearing-in as a guest of honor. Vice President Biden, who knew about my journey and is the proud husband of a teacher, showered Mr. Osterweil with much-deserved praise and gratitude.

The huge blue-and-gold compass glazed into the room's Minton tile floor and the constellation of stars painted on the high ceiling above couldn't have been a more fitting backdrop that day for the people in that room who had helped chart my life's course and light the way.

The final year of the Obama administration put every cabinet member in a race against the clock. Fervent hope that the Democrats would win again with the 2016 presidential election and send Secretary of State Hillary Clinton to the Oval Office as the first female president was pitched against the creeping dread of the potential that Donald Trump, the real estate developer and reality television star, would defeat her.

A far-right, anti-government Trump administration could undo so much of what President Obama had sought to accomplish, from dismantling Obamacare to rolling back early steps to reduce the nation's reliance on fossil fuels. In education, the progress we had made on higher standards for teaching and learning, college affordability, and civil rights protections particularly for victims of sexual assault and LGBTQ students could all be undone.

But we still had time to keep moving some critical Obama education initiatives forward. The work on turning around struggling schools continued. And the president had just signed the Every Student Succeeds Act in December 2015, which he called a "Christmas miracle" because Democrats and Republicans came together in a rare display of congressional bipartisanship. ESSA would provide funding to address the educational needs of the most vulnerable students and enforce education civil rights protections. Implementation of the new law would require the department's leadership.

In higher education, we were accelerating efforts to crack down on predatory for-profit colleges that were tricking students with empty promises and frequently worthless credentials while vacuuming up federal Pell Grant dollars, GI Bill funds the student veterans had earned serving the country, and student loan money. We were also leading cross-agency work on My Brother's Keeper, an initiative close to my heart that was designed to address the obstacles particularly impeding the success of boys and young men of color.

Believing in a policy you've helped create or implement is one thing, but meeting people that policy directly impacts, listening to their stories, and believing in *them* was a privilege. My job also meant getting to be a part of thousands of students celebrating one of the most unforgettable days of their lives: Graduation Day. Over the course of my career—from Roxbury to New York to Washington, with visits to towns and cities all across the state of New York and the United States—I have attended (and often addressed) commencements of all kinds. From kindergarteners breaking rank in the processional march to hug Grandpa to stadiums full of state-college undergrads ready to embark on careers in the real world. No matter the age, the school, or the geographical place, the overarching themes are the same: hope, promise, possibility. You'd think attending so many graduations would become tiresome, but it never has. Graduations are the best part of what I do. And the best ones, for me, happen to be in prisons.

Attending these graduations over the years captures every reason why launching the Second Chance Pell experiment was so important to me when I served as education secretary. The program was part of My Brother's Keeper and was designed to begin to correct a terrible mistake made in the 1994 Crime Bill. In that law, Congress banned access to the Federal Pell Grant program (the primary federal grant program for low-income students pursuing higher education) for students who are incarcerated. The policy was mean-spirited—an artifact of a time when mass incarceration exploded in the United States. It was just plain dumb. Overwhelming evidence shows that students who participate in educational programs while incarcerated are dramatically less likely to return to prison and therefore much more likely to contribute positively to their families, communities, and regional economy.

We knew we couldn't get Congress to change the law (yet), but we thought a pilot program could expand opportunity for the initial participants (in partnership with 60+ colleges and universities around the country) and become a model for broader change later.

As is the case with all prison graduations, just entering the room before the ceremony begins delivers an instant rush of emotion. Normal visitation days naturally come with mixed feelings, but this special visit—kids in their Sunday best, beaming parents and partners—is a chance for both the incarcerated people and their loved ones to feel nothing but pride and a giddy, unbridled joy.

For the graduates and the college professors, administrators and advisers, the day validates an effort and commitment that is truly above and beyond. Teachers must teach without many of the outside world tools to support their curriculum. Their pupils don't have unlimited access to the internet, or a college library where they can spread out their books and notes on a big wooden table and study late. For their part, the imprisoned students double down on creating their own support systems behind bars, encouraging and even tutoring one another as they all wedge pursuit of this Holy Grail of a degree into the strict regimen of a daily life where they have little agency. Skipping lunch to stay in a cell and study psychology might be an option, but there's no work-around for a noisy cellblock or the mandatory lights out at night when you have twenty more pages to read in a chapter before a quiz the next day.

Donning a cap and gown over prison khakis or a jumpsuit for one magical day and being presented with a college degree is far more than a ceremony or celebration. It's an affirmation. Over and over, I have heard incarcerated men and women acknowledge the awful choices or stupid mistakes they made, the strangers they may have harmed, the loved ones they hurt, the children they don't want to carry shame because of what they did or how society perceives them. I can easily relate to the gift of a second chance, because without the one Uncle Hal, Aunt Jean, and the teachers and school counselor at Cherry Hill West gave me when I was kicked out of Andover, the anger I felt toward adults with authority could well have landed me on a similar path of self-destruction. Mentors and teachers saved me. They gave me my career, but they also gave me my identity. In a word, they were transformative. An incarcerated man I met at Sing Sing put the transformative power of education so well when he described how devoting himself to getting a degree while incarcerated gave him "academic and moral credibility" with his family for the very first time. His classmates talked about becoming better parents because "doing school" themselves—a first for many who had dropped out young—showed them how to guide their own children.

At one graduation, where the next incoming class of Pell Grant recipients were invited to attend, I was deeply moved when I spoke about the moral obligation to pay forward one's blessings. The graduates spontaneously turned around in their seats, smiling broadly, and pointed at that next cohort of students sitting in the back in their jumpsuits.

Even with all the important work left to do in DC as the 2016 election drew closer, I traveled as much as possible to the people and places where what we sought to accomplish mattered most.

A school in Saint Paul, Minnesota, was one of those places.

Philando Castile was driving home from the grocery store with his girlfriend and her four-year-old daughter just after nine o'clock the night of July 6, 2016, when he saw the flashing lights of a police car behind him on a busy street in Falcon Heights, a suburb of Saint Paul. The thirty-two-year-old school cafeteria worker quickly pulled over and rolled down his window as Officer Jeronimo Yanez approached his 1997 white Oldsmobile. The two men greeted each other politely, and Yanez informed Castile he'd been pulled over for a broken taillight. He asked for Castile's driver's license and proof of insurance.

Seconds later, Castile was slumped in his seat covered in blood from a barrage of seven police bullets fired at point-blank range. Castile's terrified girlfriend, Diamond Reynolds, immediately began live-streaming from her cell phone, appealing for help on Facebook as the officer's gun still pointed through the window while Castile lay dying. Castile's death and the harrowing video—seen by more than 4 million viewers—sparked outrage in an ongoing national debate over racial profiling and police brutality against African-Americans, men in particular.

I went to Minnesota to visit with Castile's grieving colleagues at J. J. Hill Montessori Magnet School (a public Montessori school in Saint Paul) to express President Obama's deep concern and offer his condolences. We gathered in one of the school's common areas to talk. The people there were teachers, cafeteria workers, administrators, and parents, and mostly white.

I listened to their stories about the kind and caring man known as "Mr. Phil" to some 400 children enrolled in the school, who saw him each day at lunchtime or in the halls, holding up their hands for the high-fives he was famous for. Mr. Phil knew each child by name, along with any dietary restrictions or food allergies. When the computer system with everyone's name and lunch account number once threatened to crash, Mr. Phil hurriedly wrote the critical information down by hand, so no child unable to remember their number would go unserved. The computer also showed who had a balance due on their lunch account. Sidestepping school policy, Mr. Phil was known to quietly pay the bill from his own pocket rather than risk sending a high-needs child home without eating what could be the most nutritious or filling meal of his or her day. He was, as Diamond Reynolds tearfully insisted to the man who had just killed him, "a good man. He don't deserve this…Please! He works for the Saint Paul public schools."

Records would later show that Philando Castile had been pulled over at least forty-nine times since the age of nineteen.

Most of the cases, alleging minor traffic or equipment violations, were dismissed.

As his co-workers remembered him, the shock and anger over the scenario captured by Diamond's ten-minute livestream triggered disturbing memories for some Black people in the room—myself included.

One of the cafeteria employees Philando Castile had worked with began describing a time when he had been pulled over for no apparent reason. He recounted the sharp command, white cop to Black man: "Get out of the car!"

The man rose to his feet and walked to an open space on the floor as he continued with his story. The rest of us watched, our silence tense.

"He told me to get down on my knees, hands behind my back," he said, sinking to the floor to demonstrate, hands clasped behind him as if waiting for the clink of handcuffs. I could sense the profound fear and degradation, the way power was wielded and the way it felt as a Black person.

The school employee's reenactment of being pulled over was deeply emotional, but as I looked around, I wasn't sure it was sinking in for most of the white folks. The sympathy was there, for certain, but not empathy. I, on the other hand, could feel his fear in every fiber of his being, because I had been in that situation more than once myself.

When I had first seen Diamond Reynolds's viral video the day of the shooting, it immediately unleashed memories for me of a time in Florida when I was going slightly over the speed limit on Interstate 95 in a rental car, en route from the Orlando Airport to visit Gil in Jacksonville. Police pulled me over. First there was one squad car, then three more police cars drove up behind the first. A K-9 officer emerged from one with dogs. I was told gruffly to "Get out of the car and take everything out of the trunk." I obeyed without question, too scared things would escalate. I had assumed I was getting a speeding ticket, which I did, in fact, deserve. But now they were putting a dog in the trunk to sniff—for drugs? They told me to empty my suitcase by the side of the road and not move. I stood there, a man of color alone at night on the side of the road, surrounded by police with dogs. I was humiliated, frightened, and vulnerable.

Afterward, one of the policemen told me that the reason they had asked me to empty the suitcase was because a dog had alerted them, and they thought that previously drugs had been transported in the rental car. I didn't get a ticket. But I was acutely aware in those unpredictable minutes that I could end up falsely arrested, or used as a punching bag, as a gang of white Los Angeles policemen had done with Rodney King (another video, seared into my memory at sixteen). Or worse. I knew the first rule of survival was to just try to follow every direction a police officer gives you as carefully as you can.

Philando Castile had known that, too. In Diamond's video—and later, in the police dash-cam video played during the trial where Officer Yanez was acquitted of all charges—Mr. Phil first exchanges pleasantries with the twenty-eight-year-old Hispanic officer. As he prepares to retrieve his driver's license, he volunteers that he has a weapon in the car, which, in fact, he was licensed to carry. The dash-cam transcript captures their exchange:

> **Castile:** Sir, I have to tell you I do have a . . .
> **Yanez:** OK.
> **Castile:** . . . firearm on me.

Yanez: OK.

Castile: I (inaudible)

Yanez: Don't reach for it then.

Castile: I'm, I, I was reaching for...

Yanez: Don't pull it out.

Castile: I'm not pulling it out.

Reynolds: He's not.

Yanez: Don't pull it out!

Yanez then pulls out his weapon and opens fire into the Oldsmobile. Five bullets hit Philando.

As Mr. Phil moans, his breathing heavy and ragged, Diamond begins live-streaming, her voice with the measured, careful calm of a Black person in fear of their life holding fast to the first rule of survival. She addresses Yanez as "sir," uses the word "please." She repeats her truth repeatedly without raising her voice: "Philando was licensed to carry a gun, you told him to get his ID, sir, his driver's license, you shot four bullets into him, sir, you killed my boyfriend."

The parents knew Mr. Phil's story, they had seen the video, and now they had heard his colleague tell his story of how the intersection of race and policing sometimes played out in their community, but it was when a white administrator spoke up that the mood in the room palpably changed.

"You know, I never had any interaction with the police for my entire life until I started dating a Black man, who is now my husband," she volunteered. She was flabbergasted by how frequently he got pulled over without cause. The murmurs of dismay, heads shaking in disgust over the racial profiling of her husband, shifted the vibe in the room. On the one hand, I felt relieved, but on the other hand, it was disheartening to see that white validation was required in that moment for white people to fully connect with a Black man's anguish. But sometimes the waters can't be crossed without a bridge.

The hours I spent at the school that day were harrowing.

As I was leaving, a white parent approached.

"You know, I think the way my kids have understood race in America is that things were bad, Martin Luther King Jr. came, and now everything is good," the parent said. "I really need to help them understand that that's not true—that race in America is a lot more complicated, and there's still a lot of work to do."

He was right. And schools are uniquely positioned to cultivate empathy. I remember President Obama once telling a group of young people we met with that part of the power of reading is the opportunity to see the world from a different perspective, to literally inhabit the worldview of the narrator of a novel or the subject of a biography. Similarly, I had seen, as a teacher and as a student, how a classroom debate, a role play, or digging into a first-person account of a historical event could transform how you understood a situation by compelling you to see it from a different perspective. That is the healing power of school; school is a place that builds understanding, that transforms. That conversation at Mr. Phil's school that day changed the people in the room; in his life and, tragically, in his death, Mr. Phil was a teacher for his students, his community, and the nation.

My career as an educator in public service has made me fluent in the language of policy and politics, and the brisk shorthand—high-need, underserved, at-risk, low-performing—for our own failure as a society to provide every child an equal chance to thrive. Visiting the Pine Ridge Reservation in South Dakota, some 3,500 square miles encompassing what is often ranked as the poorest county in the country, I saw firsthand what no bureaucratic lexicon can ever adequately describe: a place with a palpable sense of hopelessness.

At the time, the reservation was home to roughly 19,000 members of the Oglala Lakota Nation, with the largest cluster—3,468—living in Pine Ridge, the tribe's administrative center. The remote reservation chronically struggled with 80 to 85 percent unemployment, sometimes even higher in winter when brutal conditions on the Plains made travel difficult. There was no public transportation, and not many people could afford vehicles. There was a single grocery store—in the town of Pine Ridge—but no banks or drugstores or any of the other conveniences and amenities of daily life. The nearest town with shopping, services, and health care was Rapid City, some 120 miles away. Chronic health conditions such as diabetes, asthma, and bronchial infections were rampant on the reservation, and with regular care too difficult to access financially and geographically, what was treatable too often turned fatal.

That year had seen a huge spike in homicides which the FBI linked to the influx of meth that cartels were smuggling onto the reservation from Colorado, some 300 miles away. Sex trafficking, assaults, and women who went missing without a trace also spread fear across a terrain too vast for tribal police to adequately patrol or protect. There'd been a rash of teen suicides lately, and everyone was worried.

It was one of the saddest places I've ever been, but...

In the tiny town of Pine Ridge itself, I met with teachers and students at Red Cloud Indian School, a private K–12 campus named for a tribal leader who foresaw education as a means of future survival for the Lakota. Back in 1888, with the federal government encroaching on tribal sovereignty, Chief Red Cloud formed an alliance with a group of Jesuits ("black robes") to create their own school for Lakota children, incorporating elements of both Catholic and Native traditions.

The school I toured over 120 years later still tightly embraced the Oglala Lakota values, heritage, and culture, weaving them through academics and the school's community life. Classes in the Lakota language and integrating it into the life of the school (later renamed Maȟpíya Lúta, which means "Red Cloud" in the Lakota language), and lessons focusing on tribal history and traditions reinforced a sense of pride and identity. I could see when they talked about the things they learned from their elders—whether it was a sun dance or the significance of different beading patterns—that the Red Cloud students felt affirmed, and a part of something. It was not dissimilar from what I'd seen as co-director at Roxbury Prep when we celebrated Kwanzaa.

When I asked the kids what they did for fun, the teens shrugged. There wasn't really anything to do, they said, except hang out. The only community rec center had closed, along with the swimming pool, which had offered a welcome break from summer temperatures that could hit 110 degrees. There were no movie theaters or skate parks. The tribe had handed out basic cell phones to everyone, but signals were often hard to get, especially when it was windy, which wasn't uncommon on the prairie, and there wasn't internet or any personal computers. A third of the reservation's population didn't even have electricity. Wood stoves were their only means to fight off winter temperatures, which could plunge below zero.

I had to listen to what the kids also weren't saying to begin to really understand their lives. I sensed from my own difficult childhood experiences that this school was likely an oasis for many. That the high rates of drug and alcohol abuse translated to volatile households, that no electricity meant no light to study by, that high unemployment meant not enough money for winter boots, that the missing girls were someone's sister, or cousin, or mother. That being part of keeping alive a language at risk of dying provided hope in a place where it was hard to find.

The high schoolers at Red Cloud Indian School talked excitedly about wanting to go to college. But their urgency wasn't the same I heard so often when I visited schools across the country and asked sixteen- and seventeen-year-olds about their aspirations and ambitions. To be so close to graduation and adulthood was to almost taste freedom, independence, a life all your own away from home. The Red Cloud kids wanted to go away to college so they could come back and make things better. For them, just as Chief Red Cloud had hoped, just as it was for the incarcerated students getting a second chance, and just as it was for me, school was a place of survival, healing, and hope.

I wanted to promise them that we would all work together to make things better. The Obama administration always asked for more money for schools on reservations and schools serving Native American students, but with a Republican Congress in the dwindling months of the president's second term, not a lot of new funding was likely to come our way. I would take their stories back to Washington with me and use their voices and their realities to advocate for more resources. Whether we would have four more years to do that, or less than four months, was about to be determined.

I decided to spend election night away from the political events and social gatherings, opting to take the family out to dinner instead to watch the results come in at Busboys and Poets, a Washington institution with a lefty vibe and, for us, a beloved neighborhood haunt. Eating at a neighborhood restaurant with a bookstore embedded in it, I anticipated a festive vibe where I could watch the election of America's first female president with my wife and daughters. But sitting at dinner and seeing the returns, I started feeling depressed as Electoral College votes foretold one of the biggest presidential election upsets in history. A pall settled over the restaurant as dejected customers began trickling out. Donald Trump was declared the winner.

The next day, people at the department were devastated. Not just the political appointees whose jobs would now evaporate, but also many of the career folks such as budget analysts and grants administrators as well. Many had worked for George W. Bush, and proudly so; their emotions weren't about partisanship. They were afraid of the vitriol, the race baiting, and the potential disregard for the rule of law and the norms of responsible governance. We all knew, though, that the work still on our desks was more urgent than ever. The Second Chance Pell experiment, for example, was up and running, with 12,000 incarcerated men and women slated to be enrolled at 67 higher education institutions across 28 states. There was important work behind the scenes channeling crucial federal investments to essential programs with life-changing impacts for students. Our efforts to stop profiteering "colleges" that were nothing but diploma mills had reached a pivotal point, and several executives running such schemes were under federal investigation. We needed to ensure we did everything we could to make their victims whole and protect future students from harm.

President Obama was the only upbeat person in the room and the most resolute when he gathered the cabinet members for one of a series of post-election events. We were going to do the transition of power "by the book," he asserted. We had to make sure the new team taking our place was as prepared as possible. We must exude confidence in America. In his tone I recognized the deep belief he held in one of his favorite Martin Luther King quotes: "The moral arc of the universe is long, but it bends towards justice."

I wasn't sure at that moment what my next step might be, but I knew my job wasn't done, and I hoped it never would be. *Strengthening* public education was just pushing the gate open so it could *transform* lives, as mine had been.

CHAPTER TWELVE

BETWEEN SCHEDULING CONFLICTS AND A HURRICANE, IT TOOK three tries for me to lock in a date to speak at the University of Maryland Eastern Shore. They had first invited me when I was secretary and now I was leading the Education Trust, a national education civil rights nonprofit dedicated to closing the achievement and opportunity gaps facing students of color and students from low-income backgrounds, and teaching education policy at University of Maryland, College Park. It was the fall of 2018 and I was to deliver the commencement address the following spring, which gave me a tantalizing stretch of lead time. I decided to do some family research to flesh out the speech I was working on.

Like many African-American families, we always assumed we would never be able to trace our roots the way the descendants of immigrants who had passed through Ellis Island might. The people brought from Africa to America in chains came with no birth certificates or passports, no tickets saying what ship they boarded or where, no written evidence of their tribes or given names before their captors Anglicized them. I knew precious little about my father, and virtually nothing about his parents or grandparents, let alone his great-grandparents. We knew my grandparents' names, and that of Estelle and Charles E. King's seven children, five had passed away due to illness or accident or worse before I was born. Only two of their sons—my father and Uncle Hal—had been present in my life. Estelle's father had been a prominent African-American preacher, and it was his belief in education that landed Estelle at Princess Anne Academy, now the University of Maryland Eastern Shore, from which she graduated in 1894. But now, the advent of the internet opened new doors for discovery in genealogical research. The historian in me yearned for more facts, the lonely child, for deeper connection. I decided to turn to an expert for help.

I reached out to archivist Christine McKay, who had uncovered boxes containing letters and documents from President Obama's father dating back a half century while she was doing research at Harlem's Schomburg Center for Research in Black Culture. Cousin Hal's efforts to fill in the family tree had yielded the name of our great-great-grandmother, Lydia Hall King, and armed with that scrap of information, Chris went to work. She spent several months combing through the Maryland State Archives, census data, and tax and property records.

I was at home, watching TV on the couch with Melissa and the girls—most likely *Friday Night Lights*, the compelling TV drama about a Texas high school football team—when a missive from Chris popped into my in-box.

I paused the show to read her email aloud. She had learned that Lydia Hall King and her husband, Reason, were both enslaved by a man named Thomas Griffith, who owned a 190-acre property called Edgehill Farm. Chris provided links to photos of the land, of Griffith's house, and the log cabin where Lydia and Reason lived with their six children born into slavery. Griffith's direct descendants still owned the property and lived in the farmhouse. The cabin, too, was still standing. The address Chris included was in Gaithersburg, Maryland.

It was just twenty-three miles from where we lived.

I was both overwhelmed by this gift of history and shocked by its intimacy. Staring at these pictures with my wife and daughters, I tried to absorb the reality of what once had been a vague assumption, shared by millions of other Black families in America. A critical lost piece of our family puzzle had just unexpectedly fallen into place, and now we had to decide what to do next. Should we write a letter to the current owners? Pick up the phone and cold-call them? Just drop by unannounced? How would an introduction even be phrased? *My name is John King, and your family enslaved mine?* Too straightforward could be read as aggressive and scare them off. Too polite ran the risk of sounding obsequious. While Melissa and I mulled semantics, Amina and Mireya, both adolescents, were curious to see what they could learn online about the property owners—a pair of sisters named Becker— hoping to assess how receptive they might be to meeting us. What if they were hostile? Meanwhile, I shared the email with my nephew Keith, Jan, Denauvo, Hal, and the rest of the cousins. Whatever happened next needed to be a family decision.

Unbeknownst to us, Jan and Denauvo were already planning to come to DC the following week for a conference and to see the new National Museum of African American History and Culture. When they reached the Slavery and Freedom Gallery,

Jan was struck by the sight of a small cabin in the middle of the room. The Point of Pines Slave Cabin exhibit is a rectangular weatherboard building, one story, standing just 73 inches tall, about 20.5 feet wide and 15.5 feet deep. There is a gabled roof with an overhang above the tiny porch, and a brick chimney. Built in 1853 on Edisto Island, South Carolina, the cabin had been occupied by Black families—from enslavement through emancipation all the way up to home ownership in the late twentieth century. It was placed on the National Register of Historic Places in 1986. After finishing their tour of the museum, Jan and Denauvo got into their car to head home to North Carolina.

Jan suddenly announced, "I need to see this place." Denauvo knew she meant Edgehill Farm in Maryland, and he wondered aloud whether they shouldn't call ahead, wait for an invitation. "We'll be just fine," Jan assured him. It took about an hour to get there. They knocked on the door of the old white farmhouse. A ramshackle smokehouse and old log cabin stood in the yard, just steps away.

"Hello," Jan greeted the woman who appeared in the doorway. "My name is Janis King Robinson, and I'm really sorry to interrupt your day, but we've recently been informed that our ancestors were enslaved here."

Frances Becker was stunned. She had been expecting to see someone responding to her Craigslist ad offering fifty-gallon water barrels for sale. Her family had never even considered the possibility that anyone related to the people their great-great-great-grandfather kept enslaved 150 years ago would show up one day.

"Well," Frances responded, opening the door wider, "come on in."

Jan called me from the car after their impromptu visit. I was impressed that she had been so bold. She filled me in, describing Frances Becker and her twin sister, Amanda, as nice, and very open. Jan and Denauvo had seen the cabin, which was used now to store old furniture and farm equipment. When her hosts kept using the word "slave" to describe the cabin, its inhabitants, and the cemetery some were buried in on the property, Jan spoke up. "Enslaved person is better," she corrected them. It restored humanity that the word "slave" purposefully erased, acknowledging them as people rather than property.

Frances took the gentle rebuke well. "I'm a work in progress," she told Jan.

The visit had left Jan with a feeling she described as profoundly spiritual. She was certain she was meant to be in that place on that day, drawn there by a force more powerful than curiosity or an intriguing email. The Beckers had provided their contact information, inviting her to stay in touch.

The official state "slave census" Chris found indicated that we were related to as many as a dozen, and perhaps all fifteen, enslaved men, women, and children considered the property of Thomas Griffith. Though it was a slaveholder state, Maryland had never seceded; it remained in the Union, and as such, was exempted from President Lincoln's Emancipation Proclamation, which went into effect in January 1863. That bit of politicking cost tens of thousands of Black people more than another year of enslavement, until a new state constitution formally abolished slavery. The state's Record of Slaves in Montgomery County at the Time of the Adoption of the Constitution in 1864 is a handwritten ledger with labeled columns: Name of owner, name of slave, sex, age, physical condition. My great-great-grandmother was at the top of Griffith's list. Lydia had been the oldest in the cabin then, at fifty. She was described as healthy. A separate tax record assessed her value at $600. The youngest person under Griffith's entry was a nine-year-old girl named Lucy King. Under a column labeled "Term of Servitude," the words "For life" were written after each name.

We emailed the Beckers and set a date to visit. The ensuing weeks would bring lessons from the most unexpected of teachers: my ancestors, who had survived the indescribable cruelty of the institution of slavery because of their faith in a future they could not see.

The rural road leading to the farm is deeply shaded, twisting its way for miles past woods and pastureland, houses largely hidden from view by trees or cornfields; Griffith Road is named for one of the county's founding families, and biggest property owners. Their heirs were expecting us. Despite Jan's thorough briefing, I could still feel the nervous energy in the car as we drew closer to the modest white house with weathered teal shutters. The Beckers were waiting for us outside.

The twin sisters, both around my age, and their father, John, greeted us warmly, and took us on a quick walk around the farmyard to give us a sense of the layout. I was stunned to see how close the main house was to the log cabin the Beckers still referred to as the "quarters"—the tiny dwelling basically sitting in their side yard. I couldn't fathom two families occupying the same physical space, one owning the other.

The property's original smokehouse squatted in front of the cabin. It was easy to imagine chickens scratching in the dirt yard, or children running through the fields and bucolic woods. I thought of my ancestors living full lives, with families and relationships, joy and sadness, yet their experiences bound up with their exploitation. *"For life."*

We all had to duck to pass through the cabin's low, narrow doorway in single file.

The solitary room was full of discarded detritus of modern life—jumbled piles of rusted garden tools and broken chairs, a porch light, a tacklebox. We stepped around bags of fertilizer and weed killer to take in not what was there but what once was. The Beckers' casual use of the cabin as a storage shed struck a nerve, but we hadn't even begun to figure out what our relationship—if any—might look like sharing this uncomfortable history, and I kept quiet. Despite the clutter, I felt the same chill I had experienced at Elmina. Black people don't usually think they will ever be in the actual space where their ancestors were enslaved. I found it surreal.

How many generations of our family had inhabited the cabin is unclear, as is how many of our ancestors are buried in the unmarked enslaved people's burial ground in the woods, not much more than 100 yards from the cabin, where the Beckers grew up having "tea parties amongst the ghosts." We do know that my family's departure was spurred by the Civil War and the eventual end of slavery in Maryland. My great-grandfather, Charles, left Edgehill Farm at twenty along with his two brothers, all three joining the military to fight in the Civil War. At the same time, an article by a local historian stated that their fifteen-year-old sister—my great-great-aunt, Annie—reported seeing her enslaver entertain "a nicely dressed stranger," which resulted in Thomas Griffith's arrest and prosecution for aiding "a known rebel officer." (Amina and Mireya loved that story and the image of their fifteen-year-old ancestor Annie bravely standing up to her oppressor.) My great-great-grandmother Lydia lived to see freedom at the age of fifty and was described as a widow with a "light brown" complexion in the records of Freedman's Bank, which offered services to the emancipated Black people after the Civil War. Charles King returned from his service in the military and ended up in New York, where he worked as a porter and married my great-grandmother, Julia. There was nothing in the research we had to tell me whether Julia, too, had once been enslaved. She gave birth to my grandfather, Charles E. King, who appeared to have been an only child. He married my grandmother Estelle Stansberry in June 1904, and they settled in Brooklyn. Her determination to see that her sons John, Hal, and Dolly went to college profoundly shaped my life and the lives of my cousins.

Our family journey across the twenty-three miles from that cabin in Gaithersburg to our home in Silver Spring was nothing short of extraordinary. In the commencement address at University of Maryland Eastern Shore, I explained, "The slave 'quarters' [cabin] is just feet from the main house. Seeing that, I was struck that there could be such intimacy in oppression. Struck by the cruelty and exploitation of which human beings are capable. At the same time, I also was struck with a profound sense of hopefulness. Yes, *hope*. My great-grandfather grew up enslaved before the Civil War. And three generations later, his great-grandson— the man standing before you—served in the cabinet of the first Black president of the United States. In this story, and so many others like mine, there is a sense of the degree to which America is always... becoming. Continuously striving. Reaching to attain her highest ideals. Striving to be truer to the founding principles of equality and democracy."

In my own life, I had gone from the darkness and despair of my bedroom in Brooklyn to the peace and joy of a family I cherished and a career I loved. Teachers had given me the hope to go on, to believe things could be better. I only speculate about where my ancestors, deprived not just of material comforts but of their very freedom and human dignity, drew that hope. Maybe they found it in the Bible, or in the simple pleasures of family life, but their perseverance made my life possible. My daughters and I *are* because they survived.

As I reflected on my frustration seeing so much of our good work in the Obama administration undone, my horror at the cruelty of immigrant children put in cages, voting protections stripped away, Black lives wrongly taken by police violence, and my outrage at the sense that American democracy was slipping backward, I drew strength from my ancestors. I felt blessed to have had the opportunity to stand inside that cabin not just to mourn the depth of my family's suffering, but to celebrate the intensity of their resolve and the triumph of their vision.

The Becker family had been on a journey, too.

After our visit to the cabin and a bit of exploring the grounds, we were invited back to the main house, where the Beckers served us refreshments. John Becker turned out to be a retired Montgomery County schoolteacher who had been born and raised in the Bronx. When we mentioned that our girls were in Montgomery County schools, he lit up and began sharing memories from his classrooms. I felt the instant bond I always did with teachers who loved the job as I did. Frances and Amanda clearly loved history and were well versed in details about their antique-filled home's construction and the relatives who had lived there. They considered it their patriotic duty to honor the ones who had worn Confederate uniforms to battle in the Civil War. They showed us a chair that had been at the Maryland Constitutional Convention. A piano in the parlor led to a cherished portrait of the great-grandmother who the Beckers described as so beautiful that Union soldiers passing by couldn't help but stop at the window and marvel at her beauty as she played "Dixie"—the anthem of the Confederacy—on her piano.

"We hope our family wasn't cruel to your people," one of the sisters ventured. She sounded sincere, but I couldn't offer the platitudes she surely wanted.

"I know you hope they didn't physically torture my ancestors," I said, "but slavery *is* torture; owning human beings is torture." They nodded.

As we prepared to say our goodbyes to the Beckers, both sides clearly felt the same tentative start of a relationship with no template, and we urged each other to stay in touch. "We're thinking we might start using the pool again," one of the Beckers told Mireya and Amina. "Come over, bring your friends!"

Back in the car, we tried to absorb and process what had just happened, as if we had just left a compelling movie with an ambiguous plot. Should we foster a relationship? What would that look like? What would it become over time? What obligations, if any, did we have to each other? The pool party gesture left all of us perplexed. How would the girls introduce the Beckers to their friends, or explain how our families knew each other, or why we were driving over to use their pool?

Some of our friends, when we had told them about finding the slaveholder's descendants, said we should ask for reparations, that we were owed something for the suffering of our ancestors. The Beckers would later confide that they feared as much before meeting us, that we just wanted something.

But truth was, Melissa and I reasoned, our house was nicer than theirs. We had more education, more income. Frances Becker sold vintage auto parts; Amanda, the other sister, had run a cemetery restoration business with her husband. Did I want something? Yes. Did I know what that was? No, but I was sure it wasn't money.

After that first visit, the Beckers emailed to let us know they had cleaned out the cabin; they were excited to show us. Frances invited me to speak at her chapter of the United Daughters of the Confederacy, a club for female descendants of Confederate soldiers with a long history of myth building around the Civil War. Since its founding in 1894, the organization had championed the "Lost Cause" version of history that tries to reframe the Confederate cause as a heroic fight for states' rights rather than for the preservation of the institution of slavery. For decades, the Daughters of the Confederacy promoted the Ku Klux Klan and romanticized their devotion to white supremacy, even trying to frame the KKK as some sort of noble resistance to Northern domination of the South. The invitation was genuine and came from a good place, but I explained to Frances that I had to decline because I didn't want to in any way legitimize the ugly legacy of the organization. She seemed sincerely surprised and said her involvement had been focused on maintaining the history of the region and delivering medals to veterans descended from Confederate soldiers.

A similar clash over history occurred when we invited the Beckers to our house for brunch. Melissa's dad, Biff, happened to be visiting. The sisters arrived, along with Amanda's husband. This was at a time of increased public awareness arising from the Black Lives Matter movement leading to demands for local governments to remove Confederate symbols such as statues and plaques from public land. Frances explained that she had been upset that a bronze statue of a Confederate soldier modeled after a relative had been removed. The Beckers wanted to know what I thought.

"Well, I think they should be taken down," I said. "They represent defending and preserving slavery, and I don't think you should glorify that."

The Beckers countered that they were merely honoring their ancestors for their military service, not for the cause they were defending. I knew they weren't trying to bait me; they just didn't understand. Biff jumped in.

"You know, many of these statues of Confederates were put up in the twentieth century in response to moments of civil rights progress," he pointed out. "They're less about honoring people who died and more about sending a message about racial hierarchy in our society." The Beckers acknowledged that Biff's observation was something they needed to think more about.

We have continued to exchange visits with the Beckers over the years. When Frances traveled to North Carolina with friends, she made time to visit Jan at her home. When John Becker died, we went to his funeral and paid our respects. We consider them friends. And that friendship has challenged me to think more deeply about America's divisions around race. The Beckers are genuinely warm and loving people. They, of course, do not bear any personal moral responsibility for the actions of their ancestors, and they themselves hold the values of equality and justice dear. Yet the fact that before meeting us, the Beckers had not reflected more deeply on the institution of slavery while growing up amid its artifacts is telling about the work we have not yet done as a country. The truth is they and we are inheritors of a society profoundly shaped by the institution of slavery and its legacy. Although some would have schools hide that truth and other ugly truths of America's past, to move forward as a country requires reckoning with our full history: both the triumphs of our progress toward fulfilling the promise of "life, liberty, and the pursuit of happiness" in the Declaration of Independence *and* the tragedy of the times we have fallen short. The relationship we Kings have built with the Beckers is forged with honesty and reconciliation, a beacon for me about what is possible for our society if we listen to each other with caring.

———————

As an educator, I am constantly learning and relearning from the teachers, mentors, and role models who have shaped my life, some alighting for a moment, others staying forever. Some have been amazing classroom teachers like Mr. Osterweil and Miss D, others have been mentors like Greg Johnson at PBHA and Harry Streep at Beacon High School, while still others have been people whose lives I have been lucky to have intertwine with mine, like the countless students I have taught and colleagues I have worked with. My family, from my parents to my Uncle Hal and Aunt Jean to Melissa and the girls, have gifted me with love and profound insights. Sometimes the teachers have been friends like Eric, Evan, Teresa, and even the Beckers. Each lesson each of these teachers offers adds not just to what I know, but to who I am—who we all are.

I'm the same age now that my great-great-grandmother Lydia was when she finally tasted freedom. Each time I leave Edgehill Farm to head home, I understand that the distance between the two cannot be measured by the mile or the milestone.

I've learned that life's journey unfolds in a much more extraordinary way, teacher by teacher.

ACKNOWLEDGMENTS

In addition to expressing gratitude beyond words to my family (Melissa, Amina, and Mireya) for their extraordinary patience as I juggled family responsibilities, a very full professional life, and the book project, there are a number of people whom I must thank for helping to make this book a reality.

I am grateful to Tamara Jones, Gail Ross, and Krishan Trotman (along with the entire Legacy Lit team) for their faith that mine was a story worth telling.

My fourth-, fifth-, and sixth-grade teacher, Mr. Osterweil—who literally saved my life—was incredibly generous with his time in helping to reconstruct those crucial years in my life. I will never be able to thank him enough for what he has meant to me.

I deeply appreciate the family (Melissa, Jan, Keith, Hal) and friends (Eric, Evan, Josh, Teresa, Kate) who sat for long interviews to help flesh out my recollections.

Acknowledgments

While I describe many critical teachers and mentors in the pages of this book, I couldn't name them all. To those named and unnamed, please know I am eternally grateful.

Finally, thank you to the DEY. and SquadBuck teams for their help getting the word out—not just about the book, but about the extraordinary debt of gratitude we owe the teachers in our lives and the urgent need to cultivate the next generation of diverse, inspiring, engaging, and dedicated educators.

ABOUT THE AUTHOR

John B. King Jr. served in President Barack Obama's cabinet as the tenth US Secretary of Education. Over the course of his extensive and influential career in public education, he has been a high school teacher, a middle school principal, the first African-American and Puerto Rican to serve as New York State Education Commissioner, a college professor, and the president and CEO of the Education Trust, a national education civil rights organization. King is currently the chancellor of the State University of New York (SUNY), the nation's largest comprehensive system of public higher education. King and his wife, an education researcher and former elementary school teacher, have two daughters, and they live in Brooklyn, New York.